The Life and Miracles of Saint Philomena, Virgin and Martyr was retrieved from the website saintsbooks.net and is in the public domain according to the site's following statement:

"The books and extracts sought for provision in the Saints' Books library are from the public domain or copyright retained but permission to be freely redistributed e-texts."

Introductory commentaries, images, and hyperlinks for the Kindle e-text were added by Walter Adams, Joan and Thérèse Publications.

The Life and Miracles of Saint Philomena, Virgin and Martyr

This is understood by the publisher to be a book in the public domain as retrieved from the website saintsbooks.net. This edition has been enhanced by the publisher with introductory commentaries to aid individual meditation or group discussion as well as hyperlinks for the Kindle version to aid with navigation.

All profits from this book are donated to the National Shrine of St. Philomena in Briggsville, WI, her home shrine in Mugnano, Italy, her Confraternity, or to any charitable cause contributing to spreading devotion to St. Philomena. No profits are retained for the personal use of the publisher. This book is published and sold solely for the glory of St. Philomena.

Joan and Thérèse Publications

Walter Adams

Table of Contents

THE LIFE AND MIRACLES OF SAINT PHILOMENA, VIRGIN AND MARTYR 3
- PUBLISHER'S INTRODUCTION 7
- PERSONAL TESTIMONY 10
- ON THE MANNER IN WHICH THE MATERIAL IS PRESENTED 12
- THE GREAT MERIT OF DEVOTION TO ST. PHILOMENA 14
- PRAYER OF CONSECRATION TO ST. PHILOMENA 17

THE LIFE AND MIRACLES OF SAINT PHILOMENA, VIRGIN AND MARTYR 21

INTRODUCTION. 23

TO THE READER. 25

THE LIFE AND MIRACLES OF SAINT PHILOMENA, VIRGIN AND MARTYR 27

INTRODUCTION. 27

CHAPTER I. DISCOVERY OF THE BODY OF ST. PHILOMENA. 39

CHAPTER II. HISTORY OF THE MARTYRDOM OF SAINT PHILOMENA. 45

CHAPTER III. TRANSLATION OF THE RELICS OF ST. PHILOMENA TO MUGNANO, AND THE MIRACLES THAT FOLLOWED. 65

CHAPTER IV. MIRACLES WROUGHT IN FAVOR OF CHILDREN. 76

CHAPTER V. FAVORS GRANTED THROUGH THE INTERCESSION OF ST. PHILOMENA. 85

CHAPTER VI. EXAMPLES OF A JUST SEVERITY EXERCISED BY SAINT PHILOMENA AGAINST THE IMPIOUS. 95

CHAPTER VII. PRACTICES OF DEVOTION IN HONOR OF ST. PHILOMENA. 102
- FIRST CONSIDERATION. 104
- SECOND CONSIDERATION. 104
- THIRD CONSIDERATION. 105
- FOURTH CONSIDERATION. 106
- FIFTH CONSIDERATION. 107
- SIXTH CONSIDERATION. 108
- SEVENTH CONSIDERATION. 109
- EIGHTH CONSIDERATION. 110
- NINTH CONSIDERATION 112

PRAYERS. 116

PRAYER. 122

PRAYER TO ST. PHILOMENA. 123

ANOTHER NOVENA TO SAINT PHILOMENA. 126
First day. 126
Second day. 126
Third day. 127
Fourth day. 127
Fifth day. 128
Sixth day. 128
Seventh day. 129
Eight day. 130
Ninth day. 130
A PRAYER IN HONOR OF ST. PHILOMENA FOR EACH DAY OF THE NOVENA. 132
For Monday, ... 135
For Tuesday. 135
For Wednesday. 136
For Thursday. 136
For Friday. 137
For Saturday. 138
LITANY IN HONOR OF SAINT PHILOMENA. 139

Personal Testimony

In the summer of 2006, I found myself faced with the greatest spiritual, physical, mental, and emotional crisis of my entire life. At the feet of a statue of the Blessed Virgin Mary while on a silent retreat in an old, abandoned seminary, I was healed completely and in an instant, mind, body, and soul. I attribute this healing, by God's grace of course, to Our Lady, St. Joan, and St. Thérèse. I have no doubt that St. Philomena was involved as well, as she has brought such an abundance of blessings to our household in the aftermath. St. Philomena truly is a miracle worker.

I will briefly relate how she has helped us in times of financial difficulty; however, keep in mind that the miracles for which the saints intercede on our behalf are not intended simply as "giving us all the things we wish for" without any spiritual intention. All of our requests for assistance must be grounded in a repentant, faith-filled heart and for the intention of bringing glory to God, improving our relationship with him, and bringing about the reign of the Immaculate Heart of Mary. We pray for material help that in receiving it, we might advance the Kingdom of God "on earth as it is in Heaven."

To this end I found myself in quite difficult financial circumstances in the Fall of 2008. Employment opportunities were few and remained out of reach. We made our way through the next few years, but at the expense of much of our savings. Finally, in March of 2012, grounded. St. Philomena was, as I suddenly realized, the perfect embodiment of my own model, which I believe was inspired by the most Holy Virgin Mary, through the Holy Spirit's guidance and the sharing of St. Joan and St. Thérèse's spiritual gifts. The Platonic ultra-realism of the early Church Fathers, such as St. Augustine, whereby we "believe in order to understand" as opposed to the more skeptical insistence that we must understand before we believe, is perfectly modeled in the life of St. Philomena as you will no doubt find when reading the beautiful account of her story here as told by those who were closest to the events of her discovery in 1805.

Thus, my goal in presenting this public domain work is foremost to bring others to a powerful devotion to St. Philomena. My own commentaries, poor and insufficient as they might be, are to demonstrate just how Philomena is indeed our perfect model and Queen for Mystical France in the center of the Immaculate Heart of Mary. My greatest fear is that what I add might in any way detract from her story. The testimony of others as related in this book requires no supplement, particularly none as modest as mine. I simply trust in our good Queen Philomena's charity, and pray that she will intercede with God Our Father in Heaven, through Jesus Christ his Son, in the power of the Holy Spirit, that others will be blessed.

St. Philomena, pray for us!

role in the latter's canonization in the 19th century. Because of Pauline's work, devotion to Philomena spread through France. The young Greek Princess is indeed very "French" in spirit!

Royaume France's model is structured as a Platonic/Augustinian understanding of France's role as The Eldest Daughter of the Church, assisted by Aristotelian/Thomist theology. It is a mystical approach to understanding the love that Our Lady, the Virgin Mary, has for the heavenly form of France as a great Catholic and Royal nation, and grounded in how one's philosophical orientation facilitates, or mitigates, our journey of faith. With St. Joan and St. Thérèse as our faithful sisters and celestial guides, Royaume France invites you to a journey on the Trail of the Dogmatic Creed to the Kingdom of God on the horizon. This journey necessarily involves our supernatural relationship with Jesus and Mary, along with our natural orientation toward belief. Grace builds on nature, St. Thomas instructs us, and Royaume France is grounded on the concept that our philosophical orientation can help or hinder us in our supernatural spiritual journey.

One day, it dawned on me that the idea to devote the work to St. Philomena as the "Queen of Royaume France" was more than simply a sentimental gesture, though that alone would have been sufficient. The more one studies this astonishing saint, the more one understands the importance of the very orientation upon which Royaume France was

Publisher's Introduction

For over a decade, I developed a spiritual model around my devotion to St. Joan of Arc, St. Thérèse of Lisieux, and what I call the form of Mystical France in the center of the Immaculate Heart of Mary. Very early in the project, St. Philomena appeared out of the mist, so to speak, and brought life and light to my work. Over the years, our (my wife, Josey and I) devotion to this young martyred Greek Princess flourished. We began making regular visits to her National Shrine in Briggsville WI. Though a tiny and remote shrine, it has had a significant impact on our spiritual lives.

I referenced Philomena in a few of my writings. Eventually, I felt overwhelmingly compelled to make her the Queen of Mystical France, as the favored daughter of Jesus and Mary.

My main body of work, Royaume France, obviously developed around a very French-based theme. I was delighted to discover the great devotion that the Curé d'Ars, St. John Vianney, had toward St. Philomena. So close was their relationship while the priest was on earth, that he gave her credit for all the miracles that famously drew pilgrims from all of France, and even all of Europe, to the small country parish.

Furthermore, through my readings on the saint, I discovered the Venerable French laywoman Pauline-Marie Jaricot, whose healing by St. Philomena played a decisive as I prepared a mortgage payment that I barely could cover and with even bleaker prospects for the following month, I cried out silently in my heart, as naturally as one would call on a dear friend, "St. Philomena! What am I going to do?"

Roughly two weeks later financial help arrived. The balance of the year went well; though, we certainly had little excess. St. Philomena knew to obtain for us only what we needed, not a frivolous abundance that might have drawn us seductively back into a worldly existence whereby we so easily forget our Lord and God.

About a year before we found ourselves finally able to get on our feet in a durable fashion, we faced one more financial crisis. With only a week or two remaining to make my mortgage payment, St. Philomena's help again arrived that would greatly relieve our situation. This answered prayer allowed us to make it to the point months later when the employment Our Lord and Our Lady had prepared for me finally came to fruition, and we were able to rebuild successfully from there.

In between these pronounced crises were many small ones. Josey and I found that St. Philomena was there always to assist us. At one point we thought that we might write down in a notebook all of the small miracles she obtained on our behalf. Sadly, we did not do so; however, they would be too numerous to summarize succinctly here.

On the manner in which the material is presented

Originally, my idea was to make commentaries throughout the retrieved text. I wanted to use St. Philomena's story as a means to relate and teach my own model as referenced above. Her story, as is, does, in fact, do that and in splendid fashion. As previously referenced, she is so much the model for Royaume France as to be Queen by virtue of it. Anyone who studies and contemplates Royaume France will easily see the Kingdom's concepts come alive in the life of St. Philomena.

Therefore, I hesitated. As I attempted to think through a commentary on how her life and sainthood poignantly reflected the Platonic and Augustinian ultra-realism so prominent in my own writings, the more clear it became to me that no one could possibly enhance the utter beauty of the words used by those who originally told the story. No doubt, they were hand-picked by St. Philomena! The more I struggled to "add" something to the narrative, the more garish, presumptuous, and arrogant I began to feel. The beauty of her story, through the souls hand-picked by her, are more than sufficient for our cause! This alone has been, however, a much needed lesson in humility for me.

Therefore, the story, as I understand it to be in the public domain, was edited by saintsbooks.net, and I leave that as it is. I pray that I am in no way infringing on any of the fruits of their merits, as they note that they seek books in the public domain for free distribution.

I leave, thankfully, the story of St. Philomena to speak for itself after my summary of her Queenship and a consecration prayer. Regarding her original story, I would ask of you the reader the following. I would ask that you use this book as a means to great devotion to St. Philomena and that at a minimum, you seek to understand one of the great lessons of her story and sainthood, which is, that we must seek to believe with a repentant, faith-filled heart of goodwill toward God and his saints, that we might understand his ways.

St. Philomena teaches us the importance of turning away from the skeptical secular rationalism of our modern world and toward true faith in Christ and his Mother. When we believe, we will understand. That alone is the key message of my original and much poorer work.

The great merit of devotion to St. Philomena

The following was written by Walter Adams for his work called Royaume France.

St. Philomena is our Queen at Royaume France by virtue of our decision to make her so and by our request to the Mother of God, Queen of all Queens, that we might subject ourselves to her through St. Philomena. Le Royaume, the Kingdom Blessed of St. Joan and St. Thérèse, is our heavenly treasure, and we give this treasure to St. Philomena as our Queen, sister, and patroness.

Why is Philomena such an important part of Royaume France, and why do we offer her our Kingdom? It is because she is the perfect symbol for our ultra-real philosophical orientation that "believes in order to understand," as opposed to "seeking to understand in order to believe." The first orientation is Platonic and grounded in the wisdom of St. Augustine. The latter is Aristotelian, and is an impediment to belief.

Through Holy Mother Church, we have every reason to believe in Philomena's saintly reality, despite attempts to cast doubt. The Holy Popes from Gregory XVI through St.Pius X, along with the holy Curé of Ars and St. Padre Pio, extolled her virtues and encouraged our devotion to her despite the fact that we have no history of her other than a couple of private revelations. God revealed St. Philomena as a mere set of bones and a vial of dried blood. Miracles abounded after her discovery, leading to holy devotion to her. In the following twentieth century, skeptics decided that she was not who the Church said she was, due to the hypothesis that the stones making up the name on the crypt were disordered purposefully as a sign that the crypt was being reused and the person inside was not the same as the one named. This deduction cast "reason to doubt" (Aristotelian) on the popes and holy saints who previously had declared with faith that we had "reason to believe" (Platonic).

As ultra-realists (Platonic) of the French Catholic Diaspora, we see Philomena's earthly presentation as the perfect symbol for our cause. Some writers have referred to her as our most powerful intercessor after Mary, which is a very noble honor indeed! How could this be, especially for a saint removed from the Church's calendar due to an Aristotelian doubt about her origins? In the sense we have described, she is so very powerful. She is a stunning symbol of ultra-realist belief among those of us with goodwill.

For the Catholic Platonic ultra-realists, such as Augustine, we "believe that we might understand," as opposed to the Aristotelian orientation to "understand before we believe." With St. Philomena, we have every reason to believe and to seek our understanding from that belief. Our Lord Jesus Christ could not have presented us with a more noble exercise in faith. In this sense, Philomena, through the eyes of faith, is truly "powerful in heaven" as our Queen, sister, and patroness. We obtain great merit by submitting to her Queenship.

Prayer of consecration to St. Philomena

The following was written by Walter Adams for his work called Royaume France.

I am eternally grateful to our most august Queen the Virgin Mary who has drawn me over the course of my life through the loving care of St. Thérèse and St. Joan, along the Trail of the Dogmatic Creed of the Roman Catholic Church, toward a Kingdom I was told to seek in the center of Mary's Immaculate Heart. Here is where St. Philomena, powerful before God and "beloved above all others"(Fr. Paul, 1954, p. 91), sits reigning as my sovereign and the protector of the treasury of graces that God, our Holy Father in Heaven with His Son our Lord and Savior Jesus Christ and the Holy Spirit, has granted to me, a most unworthy man, through the Immaculate Heart of Mary and the saintly, sisterly care of St. Joan and St. Thérèse. As St. Joan and St. Thérèse established me on this Trail leading to the center of the Immaculate Heart of Mary, I, for the first time in my life, have something of great value to give. It is to St. Philomena that I irrevocably give it.

I ask her constant intercession to God and Our Lady for the graces of Faith, Hope, and Love; Humility and Purity; Confidence; Poverty and Simplicity; Patience and Fortitude; Final Perseverance; the Seven Gifts of the Holy Spirit; Martyrdom; and all the graces I need to be a saint.

The Life and Miracles of St. Philomena, Virgin and Martyr
The original text

The life and miracles of saint Philomena, Virgin and Martyr

Whose sacred body was lately discovered in the catacombs at Rome, and from thence transferred to Mugnano, in the kingdom of Naples. Translated from the French.

"Ye dry bones, hear the word of the Lord. Thus saith the Lord God to these bones: Behold, I will send spirit into you, and you shall live." Ezech. xxxvii. 4, 5.

New York: P. O'shea, Publisher, 104 Bleecker Steeet. 1863.

This version was edited and prepared by saintsbooks.net

Approbation.

The present work being extracted from larger works, printed in Italy with the approbation of the ecclesiastical authority, and having been examined by theologians worthy of our confidence, we permit the printing and circulation of it in our diocese, referring, however, on this matter, to the declarations of the author, and especially to the decree of Urban VIII. We believe, moreover, after the example of many of our colleagues in the episcopacy, that we second the designs of Divine Providence, by recommending to the faithful of our diocese the devotion to the blessed Thaumaturga, Philomena, virgin and martyr, persuaded that it will produce, as it has done elsewhere, the most abundant fruits of sanctification.

Given at Friburg, in our Episcopal House, the 14th of July, 1834.

+ PETER TOBIAS, Bishop of Lausanne and Geneva.

J. X. FONTANA,

Chancellor of the Bishopric.

Introduction.

The name of the glorious virgin and martyr, Saint Philomena, is not as well known to the youth of our country as it should be. From the beginning of the present century, this saint has been singularly honored in Italy as the patroness of youth, and the fruits of this devotion have been truly miraculous.

The present reprint is from an authorized Dublin edition; we had hoped to have the holy privilege of translating the life of this youthful saint, but we found others had anticipated us in the pious undertaking.

The extraordinary devotion of one of the most celebrated personages of modern times -- the Cure d'Ars -- to this saint, lends a new and holy charm to her name, while its amazing fruits show how powerful she is with God. His biographer tells us that the cure's devotion to this holy virgin and martyr, whom he was accustomed to call his "dear little saint" was almost chivalrous. There was the most touching sympathy between them. "She granted everything to his prayers; he refused nothing to her love. He set down to her account all the graces and wonders which contributed to the celebrity of the pilgrimage of Ars. It was all her work; he had nothing whatever to do with it." Speaking of this devotion of the cure. Dr. Manning, the present Archbishop of Westminster, says: "Mysterious and wonderful is the sympathy which thrills through the communion of saints, unbroken by distance, undimmed by time, unchilled by death! 'The youthful saint' went forth from her mother's arms to die for Christ; the lictor's ax cropped the budding lily, and pious hands gathered up and laid it in the tomb; and so fifteen centuries went by, and none on earth thought upon the virgin martyr who was following the Lamb whithersoever He went, till the time came when the Lord would have her glory to appear; and then He chose a champion for her in the lonely, toil-worn priest, to whom He had given a heart as child-like, and a love as heroic as her own; and He gave her to be the helpmate of his labors, and bade her stand by him to shelter his humility behind the brightness of her glory, lest he should be affrighted at the knowledge of his own power with God."

We trust this little volume will serve to enkindle a tender devotion to the saint in many a young heart. At the early age of thirteen years, this true heroine trampled all the vanities of the world under her feet, and chose to endure multiplied torments rather than renounce her vow to her crucified Saviour. What a model of constancy and of every virtue does she present to us! Let the youthful heart go to her when tried, and with un- bounded confidence implore her intercession!

Mount St. Vincent, Feast of St. Philomena, August 10th, 1865.

To the reader.

This work has been composed at the instance of a venerable prelate. The greater, part of what it contains has been extracted from two works, written in Italian, on the great saint, of whom it is a panegyric. These two works were submitted to the ecclesiastical authority before publication; and that one, of which I have principally made use, bears upon it the permission to publish, of the holy office, under date of December 12, 1833. The other, of which the first is but an abridgment, contains this passage: "The name of St. Philomena is sounded everywhere with glory; devotion to her wins the hearts of all. Bishops, archbishops, princes of the Church, * the old, the young, all, even disbelievers, and the very impious, whose eyes are opened by the works of Thaumaturga, are anxious to render her homage.

There might be added, the Sovereign Pontiffs themselves, Leo XII. having proclaimed her the great Saint; and Gregory XVI. has recently blessed one of her images, destined to receive public devotion, in the capital of Christendom.

I have heard bishops exclaim, 'Blessed be God, who vivifies us through St. Philomena.'" Since her devotion has been publicly established in the dioceses, there are seen persons who did not believe in the creation, seeking with humility an image of the saint, and as soon as they have obtained it, their faith rejoices, as if they possessed a treasure. What mercy God displays in this amiable saint!

But as Philomena has acquired this celebrity, merely from the recital of her miracles, communicated orally, or by writing, should we not see, in this very celebrity, a living proof of the truth of these wonders? The graces of every kind with which this proof is accompanied, form a second testimony, which it is hard to resist. And if we add, that the theater of these wonders is Italy; that there, in presence of the pillar and seat of truth, the orators publish the prodigies of the saint, and the books whence they draw their information are printed and reprinted, and that the editions are quickly exhausted; shall we not, therefore, draw a conclusion decidedly in favor of what the former preach, and of what the latter contain?

I shall not, however, here omit to declare, as I am bound to do, and in accordance with the decree of Urban VIII., that I do hope pretend to give any of the facts contained in this book more authority than the Catholic, Apostolic, and Roman Church gives or will give to them, whose decision is, and shall always be, in everything the rule of my judgments.

I. F. B. D. L., C. D. I.

FRIBURG, 23d of June, 1834.

The life and miracles of Saint Philomena, Virgin and Martyr

Introduction.

"Qui habet aurem, audiat quid Spiritus dicat Ecclesiis." -- (Apoc. ii. 7.) "He that hath an ear, let him hear what the Spirit saith to the churches."

The different churches or dioceses of which the Christian world is composed, form but one and the same church: Jesus Christ, our Lord, is the chief; and the Pope, his visible representative on earth, the common father of all the faithful, governs it in his name and by his authority. No one is ignorant of how this church has been formed. Before ascending into heaven, to be seated at the right hand of his Father, our Lord Jesus Christ promised his apostles to send them his Spirit, the spirit of truth, which was to instruct them; the spirit of fortitude, which was to animate them; the spirit of zeal, which was to convey them from one end of the world to the other, in order to proclaim everywhere the divinity of Jesus Christ, "and to call from the bosom of darkness to the admirable light of the gospel, this elected race, this royal priesthood, this holy nation, this people acquired," for his Heavenly Father and his angels, "by a crucified God." -- (1 Pet. ii. 9.)

The day of Pentecost arrives -- suddenly, towards the third hour, a great noise is heard, like the blast of an impetuous wind; it fills the coenaculum, * where the apostles were in prayer with Mary, the mother of Jesus; and at the same instant there appear, like so many stars, upon the head of each of them, tongues of fire, the striking symbol of what the spirit of Jesus Christ wrought in them.

Changed all at once into other men, and become generous combatants for the faith, they enter the lists, and commence that warfare which has subjected the whole earth to the empire of the Saviour, and which will terminate but with the end of the world.

Coenaculum means literally a room appropriated to eating, and is particularly used to denote the apartment in which the disciples were assembled at the time the Holy Ghost descended upon them, and that in which the last supper was celebrated. -- Transl.

"Today," cries the prince of the apostles, is accomplished what was spoken of by the prophet Joel: And it shall come to pass, in the last days (saith the Lord), I will pour out of my spirit upon all flesh; and your sons and your daughters shall prophesy, and your young men shall see visions, and your old men shall dream dreams. And upon my servants, indeed, and upon my handmaids, I will pour out in those days of my spirit, and they shall prophesy. And I will show wonders in the heaven above, and signs on the earth beneath; blood, and fire, and vapor, and smoke. The sun shall be turned into darkness, and the moon into blood, before the great and manifest day of the Lord come. And it shall come to pass, that whosoever shall call upon the name of the Lord shall be saved." -- (Acts ii. 16, &c.) What Joel had announced, what Peter publishes in the middle of Jerusalem, in presence of an immense multitude, "composed of all the nations which are under heaven " (ibid.), the history of all the ages of Christianity, even to our own days, attests the wonderful accomplishment of; so that the Catholic, Apostolic, and Roman Church can, at the present time, show to the whole world, as a living title to its veneration, prodigies of every kind, wrought in every place, by her children; Domino cooperante, et sermonem confirmante sequentibus signis; "The Lord working withal, and confirming the word with signs that followed." -- (Marc. xvi. 20.)

The life-giving Spirit, which has not ceased, and will never cease to animate it, gives to some, as St. Paul says, the gift of wisdom; to others, the gift of knowledge; to one, the grace of restoring health to the sick; to another, prophetic knowledge, that teaches him to know the future; to others, the power of working all manner of prodigies. -- (1 Cor. xii.) And the end for which this divine Spirit communicates his omnipotence to the church is, St. Thomas tells us, "that all men may come to the knowledge of God." *

Here I would be tempted to cry out with the Royal Prophet, "Lord, what is man, that thou shouldst think of him," when thou wishest to display thy glory? What then is the son of man, that, not satisfied with visiting him, thou shouldst establish him the depository of thy divine power, and, as it were, the Lord of his adorable Master?

* *Beneficium commune, quod exhibetur in omnibus miraculis, ut scilicet homines adducantur ad Dei notitiam.* (2. 2. qu. 178, art. 1 ad 4.)

For, in miracles, although the creature be not the instrument, he commands, nevertheless, and God obeys; * he wills, sometimes even he manifests only a desire, and God executes his will, realizes his wishes; thus St. Thomas expresses it, Deo ad nutem hominis operante.

But why should we wonder at favors like these, with which God has been pleased to honor his church, since, after all, they are the less precious of his gifts? "The greatest miracles," says St Gregory, "are those of the spiritual order; those which work not the resurrection of bodies, but the resurrection of souls." ** "And if God," adds St. Augustin, "has placed in reserve, in the treasures of his mercy, some of these extraordinary effects of his power, which shake man in his lethargy, and draw from him a tribute of admiration for his Creator, it is not because he desires him to regard them as greater than those of which he is every day witness, but in order to awaken, by what is rare and unusual in them, the value which the former, by their daily occurrence, had lost, in the minds of men." ***

* *Obediente Deo voci hominis. (Jos. x.)*

** *Miracula tanto majora sunt, quanto spiritualia; tanto majora sunt, quanto per haec non corpora, sed anime suscitantur. (Hom, xxix.)*

*** *Ut non majora, sed insolita vivendo stuperent, qui hos quotidiana vilucrant, &c., &c. (Tract, xxiv. in Joan.)*

Thus, though I should see a man, clothed with the divine power as with a garment, work in heaven and on earth the greatest wonders; though I should be witness of numberless cures, of resurrections as evident as multiplied, of the prompt and continual obedience which the elements, the tempests, all nature would render to the voice of this new Thaumaturgus, my heart, undoubtedly, humbling itself before God, the principal author of these prodigies, would render glory to his name, and would confess the greatness of his power; but it would remember also what St. Paul said, "That there are graces still more estimable, because they are better and of a superior order;" * "and a look of faith upon the crucifix, and upon the tabernacle where our divine Saviour resides, would be sufficient to set limit to my admiration, and make me reserve it for the infinite grandeur of these truly divine wonders.

I say this, both to answer those who deny miracles, because they believe them impossible, and to inspire a just admiration in many others, who, over desirous of hearing or of seeing these really admirable works of the Most High, become so fond of them, that everything else, no matter how sublime or divine it may be, appears to them of little value in comparison.

* *Aemulamini charismata meliora. Et adhuc excellentiorem viam vobis demonstrabo. (1 Cor. xii. 31.)*

Far be it from us to entertain these two errors, equally injurious to the goodness of God. You believe that he has loved the world to such an excess, that he has given for it his only Son; you believe that this only Son, the Word of God, God as his Father, has made himself one of us, that is to say, flesh, passible and mortal; you believe that he died on an infamous gibbet for the salvation of men, and that, in order to communicate to them the merits of his death, he is present and lives in the sacrament of his church; you believe -- shall I say? unhesitatingly -- these profound mysteries, which may be called the miracles of miracles; and those wonders which the power of God -- those works which your senses themselves attest to you -- could you doubt of their possibility? Leave these doubts to the impious; and when the Lord shows to you, by his angels and saints, the ordinary ministers of his power upon earth, that his hand is not withdrawn, and that he is always the God, to whom it alone belongs to do wonders, reply to all the objections that the enemy of his glory may suggest to you, these first words of the symbol of faith, Credo in Deum Patrem omnipotentem.

As for the other error, it will be sufficient for banishing it, to read the words of the angelical doctor. "The working of miracles," he says, "has for its end, to confirm in faith." * How, then, could it diminish the value of faith? You ought, on the contrary, as St. Augustin says, "to aid yourself by these visible works, in order to raise up your mind to the admiration of an invisible God," such as faith shows him to us in his mysteries and in his sacraments. **

This is not yet sufficient, adds the same doctor. "Interrogate the miracles themselves, to know from them what they wish to tell you of Jesus Christ; for if you could comprehend them, they have also their language." ***

Do you now, then, believe that they tell anything else, except that you should ascend still higher, and that the admiration you feel should give place to the delight with which the super eminent and infinite love of Jesus Christ ought to inspire you, in the most inestimable gifts with which he is pleased to adorn his only and well-beloved spouse, the Catholic, Apostolic and Roman Church?

* *Operatio miraculorum ordinatur ad fidei confirmationem. (2. 2. loe. cit. ad 5.)*

** *Hoc admotum sensibus, ut erigeretur mens; ut invisibilem Deum per visibilia opera miraremur, erecti ad fidem. (Tract, iv. in Joan.)*

*** *Interrogamus ipsa miracula, qui nobis loquantur de Christo; habent enim si intelligantur linguam suam. (Tract iv. in Joan.)*

After these different considerations, which I have thought it necessary to place before those who may read this little work, I approach the subject of which I have proposed to treat. The object is, as the title announces, to proclaim a Thaumaturga, * whose wonderful works have made her name celebrated throughout the world. The abbreviation of the work written on this saint by Don Francis de Lucia, from which we borrow the materials for this notice, says: "The greatest miracle, undoubtedly, of all which the Lord has wrought in favor of the holy martyr, is the astonishing rapidity with which her veneration has been propagated. Like the light, that in a few instants bounds over the measureless space between heaven and earth, the name of St. Philomena, particularly since the miraculous (and well-proved) sweat which was seen, in 1823, upon one of her statues, erected in the church of Mugnano, has reached in a few years to the ends of the world. The books that speak of her miracles, the images representing her, have been carried by zealous missionaries into China, into Japan, and to several Catholic establishments in America and in Asia. In

Europe, devotion towards her is extending, not only in the country and in the villages, but also in the most celebrated and populous cities.

* The name which, is given to the saints that God renders celebrated by a great number of miracles.

The great and the humble, the shepherds and their flocks, unite in doing her honor. At their head are seen cardinals, archbishops, bishops, heads of religious orders, and ecclesiastics, deserving consideration by their dignities, their learning and virtues. From the Christian pulpit the most eloquent orators publish her glory; and all the faithful who know her, in the kingdom of Naples particularly, and in the neighboring countries, where there are millions of them, give to her with common accord the name of Thaumaturga. "This," continues the same author, "which we see, we touch, as it were, with the hand, and which might be called the most wonderful of the miracles, makes us hope that one day, which day is perhaps not far distant, the glorious name of St. Philomena will hold a distinguished place in the Roman Martyrology, and the universal church will render to her a solemn devotion."

The hope of the author appears to be well founded. Already, in 1827, the keeper of the holy relics, Monsignor Filippo Ludovici, presented to his holiness Pope Leo XII. a copy of the second edition of the work of Don Francis de Lucia. In consequence of what the celebrated missionary,

Don Sauveur Pascali, who was present, said, the Vicar of Jesus Christ, after running rapidly over the work, and having asked many questions of Monsignor Ludovici concerning the miracles wrought through the holy martyr, appeared impressed with a high admiration for her; and, at the same time, praising God for the power which he had given her, he blessed, in the most affectionate terms, the persons who, under the protection of this great saint (these are his words), consecrated themselves, though in the midst of the world, to the practice of perfection.

From that time, the number of the devout towards St. Philomena is daily multiplied in the very center of Catholicity. I have myself witnessed, in 1832, and have seen, with my own eyes, in the pomp displayed in the fetes * which are celebrated in her honor, persons who had received from her the most signal favors. The following are extracts from two letters written from the same city by a trustworthy person, the one dated April 4, and the other May 20, 1834: --

* The word fete, taken in its original sense, having become, from its usefulness, nearly naturalized in our language, the translator, taking advantage of this circumstance, accordingly gives to it the meaning it hears in French, viz., as denoting, together with the English word feast, the public rejoicings that take place on particular and extraordinary occasions, and which generally distinguish, on the continent, the solemn feasts of the

church, and the annual return of the festivals of Patron Saints. -- Transl.

"Our St, Philomena does not cease to perform prodigies at Rome, at Ancona, at Ferrara, at Naples, and at Florence, In the last named city, the Rev. P. F., who was preaching the lent to the court of the Grand Duke, made the panegyric of the young Thaumaturga. Her devotion is extending visibly. At Caravita we have a superb picture of the saint; and we shall soon have her chapel. Every day they make of her new engravings."

"The good St. Philomena continues to obtain all sorts of favors for those who are devout towards her. To describe here the cures and other miraculous favors obtained by her intercession, would be to compose some volumes. At Rome are seen, exposed in several churches, her picture and her relics. The people go in crowds to pay them veneration; they make prayers of nine days, three days, &c. Encourage and propagate devotion to the young Thaumaturga: you will receive from it, both for yourself and for others, peculiar graces and favors."

I ought also to add as I have heard myself in Italy, that a great number of bishops, both in the kingdom of Naples and the Papal States, have ordered in their dioceses that a public devotion should be rendered to the saint, and their clergy say the mass of her and recite the office. "It is," says the above-cited author, "a debt of gratitude which they have contracted, and which they have desired to discharge, for the benefits which the saint has bestowed abundantly on their flocks."

May this work, then, which I cast, like the last farthing of the widow, into the treasury of the glorious martyr, draw upon me a look of her benevolence, and contribute to the propagation of her devotion, as well as to the manifestation of her power, in the places where her name and her glory are yet unknown.

Chapter I. Discovery of the body of St. Philomena.

The Psalmist says: "God is wonderful in His saints. The God of Israel is He who will give power and strength to His people." Blessed be God.

During nearly fifteen centuries, these sacred relics had lain buried and concealed from the world, when all at once they appear, crowned with honor and glory. Whence therefore is this prodigy? who can have wrought it, but He who dictated these words to His prophet: -- In memoria aeterna erit Justus (Ps. cxi.): "The just will be in everlasting remembrance."

The just, therefore, only deserve to be called wise; since they build not the edifice of their virtues upon the quicksands of the world, but upon the imperishable rock, upon "the mountain of God;" Fundamenta ejus in montibus sanctis. (Ps. cxi.) Oh! that the insensate inhabitants of the earth could comprehend and appreciate this language. But, be it as it may, such is the lesson that God has been pleased to give them: if their folly prevents their profiting by it, it will not, for all that, be the less truly useful for those who already walk in the straightway; and, in seeing what the Lord has done to exalt his humble servant, St. Philomena, they will feel themselves animated with new ardor, and, full of joy and hope, they will fly, with the swiftness of the eagle, in the narrow way, of which the end is life and eternal glory. The blessed body of St. Philomena was found, in 1802, on the 25th of May, during one of those annual excavations which are usually made at Rome, in those places which have been rendered sacred by the burial of the martyrs. Those excavations took place this year in the catacombs of St. Priscilla, on the new Salarian way. The first thing discovered was the sepulchral stone, which was remarkable for its singularity. It was of baked earth, and distinguished by several symbols, bearing allusion to virginity and martyrdom. They were cut with a transverse line, formed by an inscription, of which the first and last letters appeared to have been effaced by the instruments of the workmen, when endeavoring to detach it from the tomb: it was conceived in these

words: --

(FI) LUMENA, PAX TECUM FI (AT).*

* "Filumena, peace be with thee, Amen."

The learned Father Parthenio, S. J., thinks that the two last letters, FI, ought to be united to the first word of the inscription, according to the usage of the ancients, which he says was common to the Chaldeans, Phoenicians, Arabs, Hebrews; and he adds, there are some traces of it to be found even among the Greeks. But the discussions on this point must be left to the learned, and it will be sufficient for us to observe, with the same learned Father, that, "on sepulchral stones, placed by the Christians upon the tombs of the martyrs who confessed Jesus Christ in the first persecution, in place of the formula. In pace, generally more used, they put Pax tecum, which is something more lively and more animated."

The stone having been removed, the sacred relics of the holy martyr appeared, and close beside, an earthen vase of extremely thin material, one half of it broken, and the sides incrusted with dried blood. The blood, a sure sign of the sort of martyrdom which terminated the days of St. Philomena, had been, according to the practice of the primitive Church, collected by pious Christians. "When the Christians could not themselves perform this office of devotion, they had recourse to the pagans, and sometimes even to the executioners of their brethren, in order to have, together with their venerable remains, their sacred blood, offered so generously to Him, who, upon the cross, sanctified, by the effusion of His own blood, the sacrifices, the pains, and the death of His children.

Whilst they were engaged in detaching from the different pieces of the broken vase the blood that adhered to them, and that with the greatest care they gathered in a crystal urn the small particles, the persons present, among whom were some men of talent and cultivated minds, were astonished in seeing sparkle, all on a sudden, the urn upon which their eyes were fixed. They drew nearer; they viewed at leisure the wonderful phenomenon, and with sentiments of the most lively admiration, joined to the most profound respect, blessed God, "Who is glorified in His saints." The sacred particles, in falling from the vase into the urn, were transformed into various precious and shining bodies; some presenting the luster and color of the purest gold, some of silver, some appearing like diamonds, rubies, emeralds, and other precious stones ; so that in place of the matter, of which the color, in detaching it from the vase, was brown and dark, they saw only in the crystal the mingled brilliancy of different colors, like those that shine in the rainbow.

The witnesses of this prodigy were not men to doubt of what they had seen with their eyes, and examined with attention; they knew that God, particularly to those whom in heaven He loads with the riches of His glory, is not so sparing of His gifts, as that a like miracle could cost Him much. They considered it, not only in itself, as a shadow of that heavenly brightness promised in the sacred writings to the body and soul of the just -- Fulgebunt justi sicut sol . . . . et tanquam scintillae (Wisd. iii. 7), -- but also in the happy and salutary effects which it produced in their hearts. They felt their faith revive, and had they desired to compare the present and the past, they might have recalled to mind, to justify their pious belief, many similar facts: that, for example, of St. John Nepomucene, whose body, having been cast into the Muldau, was distinguished in the midst of the waters, during the night, by the brilliant light which clothed it like a garment. What is told of St. Philomena is certainly more wonderful, but yet, how far short of that miracle, of which it is the figure and the pledge, the resurrection of the body, when the elect shall be transformed into the glory of Jesus Christ!

In reading the foregoing, one must be struck with admiration at the permanence of this miraculous transformation. At the present time it excites the wonder of all who go to venerate the sacred relics. They see also, in the same urn, the same brilliant bodies, but their brilliancy has not always the same liveliness, and the colors with which they shine have at different moments different shades: at one time it is the appearance of the ruby, at another that of the emerald that predominates; again, their brilliancy is at times as it were tarnished by a light layer of ashes. Once only it was observed to disappear, and the terrified eyes of those who witnessed it saw in the sacred urn but a little ordinary earth. But this new miracle terminated as soon as the unworthy eyes of a person, who shortly afterward died suddenly, had ceased to profane the holiness of the venerable relics. O God, how the display of Thy power is at the same time amiable and terrible!

A difficulty may here present itself to the reader's mind. This prodigy, as we have called it, took place first at the moment of the extraction of the holy body from the catacombs; the eye-witnesses must have spoken of it, and consequently it must have made a noise in Rome how then has it happened that, from the 25th of May, 1802, until almost the middle of 1805, an object so worthy of all respect should, instead of being exposed upon the altars to receive the homage of the faithful, have been kept concealed and confounded with several other bodies of holy martyrs, which it had not pleased the Lord to honor in so singular a manner? But let us reflect on and admire the wise slowness, and the supernatural, as it were, circumspection of the Court of Rome, when called upon to pronounce on these extraordinary events. Let us meditate particularly on the views of Providence in regard to these sacred remains, and the difficulty will disappear. Yes; God wished, as all that has since happened concurs to prove, that this new sun, like the morning, after having shed the first light, should remain some time longer under the clouds.

Chapter II. History of the martyrdom of Saint Philomena.

The martyrdom of St. Philomena is known only from the symbols figured on the sepulchral stone of which we have spoken, and from the revelations * made by the saint herself to different persons.

At the mention of revelations let no one be scared, as it is certain that, from the beginning of the world, God has revealed to men many things which were known but to Himself alone. "He has done so," says St. Paul, "in several places, and in many ways, but above all, in these latter times by His well-beloved Son." Then, who will dare to dispute with Him the right of doing what He has done so often, or interdict Him the exercise of this right, even in our day? If the meanness of man, or his unworthiriess, is adduced as an argument against revelation, is not our God the God of boundless mercy? Man, be he ever so miserable, is he not His child, the work of His hands and of His goodness, destined to live with Him in a blessed eternity? If it should be objected, that such communications between God and man are useless, in what manner can this be proved? The learned and great Pope Benedict XIV.(**), whose words are of great value in matters of this kind, did not think so; for he is of opinion that revelations, if they are "pious, holy, and profitable to the salvation of souls, ought to be admitted in the process that takes place at Rome, for the canonization of saints." He did not regard, then, all revelations as *useless. But if, after mature examination -- if, after having consulted persons who are learned and versed in this sort of raatters -- if, even, as it has happened with these, after having submitted them to the ecclesiastical authority, permission has been obtained to publish them for the glory of our Lord and the edification of men, who will presume to say that such revelations, filled with piety and holiness, are useless or hurtful? Let not the believer merit the reproach of the Holy Spirit that is made to the impious, "of blaspheming what they know not!" I do not desire, indeed, to see imitated the imprudence of those who, at this time particularly, admit without distinction everything they hear qualified with the name of revelation; this would be, I admit, the most dangerous folly. But I must repeat with St. Paul, that every revelation, no more than every prophecy, should not be despised (***), and that we should yield a pious belief to those which, according to the rules approved by the Church and followed by the saints, bear the characters of truth. Such are the revelations of which I am about speaking in this chapter, and which are perfectly in accordance with the hieroglyphics traced upon the sepulchral stone.*

(**) De Beatif. SS. lib. 3, tom. 7, cap. 3. (***) Prophetias nolite spernere.--l Thess. v. 20.

We shall begin with the figures on the stone: The first is an anchor; the symbol, not only of strength and hope, but also of a sort of martyrdom, such as that to which Trajan condemned St. Clement, the Pope, who, by the orders of this emperor, was cast into the sea, with an anchor tied to his neck.

The second is an arrow, which, upon the tomb of the martyrs of Jesus Christ, signifies a torment, similar to that by which Diocletian tried to put to death the generous tribune of the first cohort, St. Sebastian.

The third is a palm, placed almost in the middle of the stone: it is the sign, and, as it were, the herald of a brilliant victory gained over the cruelty of the persecuting judges, and the fury of the executioners.

Underneath is represented a kind of lash, used to scourge criminals, and which was made of thongs of leather, loaded with lead: with these the bodies of the innocent Christians ceased to be bruised, only when they had been deprived of life. *

After these are two arrows, so arranged that the first points upward, and the other in a contrary direction. The repetition of this may perhaps mark a repetition of the torments, and its disposition, a miracle; such, for example, as that which happened at Mount Gargan to a shepherd, who, having shot an arrow at a bull that had fled into a cave, dedicated since to St. Michael the Archangel, saw, as well as several other persons, this same arrow return and fall at his feet.

The discovery of many of the instruments of torture employed to aggravate the sufferings of the martyrs, has enabled us to have some idea of what their anguish must have been, when the scourge made use of was either of leather, loaded with leaden balls, or chains, to the ends of which metal rings were attached.

Lastly, a lily appeared, the symbol of innocence and virginity, which, with the palm and blood-stained vase already spoken of, proclaims the two-fold triumph of St. Philomena over the world and the flesh, and invites the world to honor her, under the glorious titles of Martyr and Virgin.

We shall now examine whether these revelations agree with the different marks just mentioned. * The reader will be able to judge for himself.

* It is well to remark, 1st, that these revelations have been made to three different persons, of whom the first is a young artisan very well known to Don Francis de Lucia, who, in his work, spread by thousands of copies in the kingdom of Naples and the surrounding states, renders public testimony to the purity of his conscience and to his solid piety. The second is a zealous priest, now a canon, for whom the devotion to the holy martyr, of whom he was the perpetual panegyrist, procured the most singular favors. The third is one of those virgins consecrated to Grod in an austere cloister, about thirty years of age, and living at Naples. 2d. These three persons were unknown to each other; they have never had any communication, and inhabit countries far separated

from each other. 3d. The accounts which they have given, whether by word of mouth or by writing, fully agree as to the basis and principal circumstances, and in no place contradict the epitaph which we have just explained, and give to it, by the details, an elucidation as clear as it is edifying.

The narrative of the artisan is as follows: "I saw," says he, "the tyrant Diocletian desperately in love with the virgin Philomena. He condemned her to many torments, and continued to flatter himself with the hope that rigor would, in the end, break her courage, and force her to yield to his wishes. But seeing that all his hopes were vain, and that nothing could bend the firm resolution of the holy martyr, he fell into fits of insanity; and in the madness that then possessed him, he bewailed his being unable to have her for his wife. At length, after having tried various tortures (and he cites precisely the same as were figured on the sepulchral stone, and of which he had absolutely no knowledge), the tyrant had her beheaded. Scarcely had the order been executed, than despair seized his soul. He was then heard to cry out, 'Woe is me! Philomena will never be my spouse! She has been refractory to my will to her last breath; she is dead; how shall I be able to survive?' and, on saying these words, he tore his beard like a madman, and fell into the most frightful convulsions, and throwing himself from his throne upon the ground, he seized on with his teeth whatever came in his way, saying that he wished to be emperor no longer." Such, in a few words, is the summary of the vision with which God was pleased to honor a simple and ignorant man.

The second revelation was made to a very zealous priest, who was exceedingly devoted to St. Philomena. Don Francis says that all he has written concerning it, he has been directly informed of by the priest himself; and, moreover, that he has heard him relate it in the very church in which are deposited the holy relics of the saint. He thus narrates the manner of his revelation: "I was walking one day in the country, when I saw approach toward me a woman who was a stranger to me; she addressed me, saying, 'Is it really true that you have exposed in your church a picture of St. Philomena?' Yes, I answered; what has been told you is perfectly true. 'But,' added she, 'what then do you know about this saint? Very little: to this hour we have only been able to know of her history what may be learned from the inscription and symbols figured on her tomb; and I set about explaining them to her. She suffered me to finish, and then with vivacity replied, 'You know nothing more, then?' No; nothing else. 'There is, however, a vast deal of other things to be said concerning this saint. When they will be known people will be filled with amazement. Do you even know the cause of her persecution and martyrdom?' Nothing more. 'Well, then, I shall tell it you. It was for having refused the hand of Diocletian, who intended her for his wife; and the motive of her refusal was the vow she had made of remaining forever a virgin for the love of Jesus Christ.' At these words, filled with gladness, like one who had just heard news for which he had a long time sighed, I said to her. You do not deceive me? are you quite sure of what I have just heard you say? But where have you read this? For during several years back we have searched for some author wherein we might find some account of this saint, and our inquiries have, hitherto, been unavailing. Tell me in what book you have found all you have told me. 'In what book? said she, in a tone in which was discoverable an expression of indescribable surprise and gravity. 'Is it really to me that such a question should be asked? to me, as if I could be ignorant of it! No, surely; I do not deceive you. Yes; I know it -- I am certain of it -- believe me.' And in saying these words, I saw her disappear with the rapidity of lightning."

To this narrative, faithfully transcribed from the Italian author, I shall add some of his reflections. "The stranger," says he, "(and whom, in my opinion, it is not difficult to recognize,) speaks of the hand of Diocletian as having been offered to her by that prince, which supposes that the martyrdom of St. Philomena should have taken place during the time that Diocletian was a widower, or was on the point of becoming so by the death of St. Sirena, whom he put to death, together with his own daughter, in hatred of the faith which both had embraced. The emperor was then at Rome, where he condemned to death, at two different times, the heroic St. Sebastian." These observations, suggested by the preceding revelation, help to determine, in some measure, the epoch of St. Philomena's martyrdom, and to refute the objection which certain critics have made, founded upon the long sojourn of Diocletian in the east.

The third revelation, and the most circumstantial, is that of a nun of Naples.* We shall follow the words of the author as closely as the genius of our language will permit.

This revelation has been published after undergoing a most strict examination, instituted by ecclesiastical authority, and it being duly and fully ascertained that it bore all the marks which distinguish true revelations from false ones.

"The holy martyr had," says he, "a long time before given to this religieuse several distinguishing marks of a very peculiar protection. She had delivered her from temptations of mistrust and impurity, by which God had wished to further purify His servant; and to the painful state in which these attacks of Satan had placed her, St. Philomena had made succeed the sweetness of joy and peace. In the intimate communications which took place at the foot of the cross between these two spouses of the Saviour, the saint gave her advice full of wisdom; at one time, concerning the guidance of the community, with which this religieuse had been charged by her superiors; at another time concerning her own personal conduct. That upon which they conversed the oftenest was upon the value of virginity, the means that St. Philomena had made use of to preserve it unsullied, even in the midst of the greatest perils; and the immeasurable treasures found in the cross and in the fruit that it bears.

"These extraordinary favors, granted to a soul so impressed with a sense of its misery as to consider itself utterly undeserving of them, made her fear some illusion. She had recourse to prayer, and to the prudence of those whom God had given her to guide her conscience; and while those wise directors submitted to a slow and judicious examination the different favors with which Heaven had honored this nun, revelations of another nature were made to her by the intervention of the same Saint, whose name they all tended to make more glorious.

"The religieuse, of whom we speak, had in her cell a little statue of St. Philomena, formed upon the model of her blessed body, such as is seen at Mugnano; and more than once the entire community had remarked on the face of this same statue alterations that appeared to them to be miraculous. This circumstance had inspired them with the desire of exposing it in their church with great solemnity.

"The fete took place, and from that time the miraculous statue remains upon its altar. The good nun used to go, on the days of her communion, to return thanks before it; and one day, as she felt in her heart a great desire to know the precise epoch of the martyrdom of the saint, that, as she said, those who had devotion to her might honor her more particularly, all on a sudden her eyes were closed in such a manner that she was unable to open them, and a voice, full of sweetness, which appeared to come from where the statue was, addressed to her these words: 'My dear sister, it was the tenth of the month of August that I died in order to live, and that I entered triumphantly into heaven, where my divine Spouse put me in possession of those everlasting joys which cannot be comprehended by the understanding of man. Thus, it was for this reason that his admirable wisdom so disposed the circumstances of my translation to Mugnano that, despite of the plans arranged by the priest who had obtained my mortal remains, I arrived in that town, not on the fifth, as it had been intended, but on the tenth of August; and not to be placed with little public solemnity in the oratory of his house, as he also wished, but in the church, where they venerate me, and in the midst of universal acclamations of joy, accompanied by miraculous circumstances which made the day of my martyrdom a true day of triumph.'

"These words, which carried with them proofs of the truth that had dictated them, renewed in the heart of the nun her fears lest she should be under an illusion; she redoubled her prayers, and begged of her director to undeceive her. They wrote, therefore, to Don Francis, enjoining him secrecy on the subject, praying him to answer distinctly as to the circumstances of the revelation which regarded the resolutions he had taken. He answered that they were perfectly in accordance with the fact. This reply not only consoled the agitated nun, but encouraged her directors, for the glory of God and St. Philomena, to avail of this means which the saint herself seemed to point out, in order to acquire circumstantial information concerning her life and martyrdom.

"They therefore commanded this said person to use for this purpose the most earnest solicitation with the saint, and as obedience, according to holy writers, is always victorious, one day, when she was in her cell, in prayer to obtain this favor, her eyes closed as before, in spite of resistance, and she heard the same voice, which said to her, "My dear sister, I am the daughter of a prince who governed a small state in Greece. My mother was also of royal blood; and as they were without children, and they both still idolaters, in order to obtain some, they used continually to offer to their false gods sacrifices and prayers. A doctor from Rome, named Publius, now in Paradise, lived in the palace in the service of my father; he professed Christianity. Seeing the affliction of my parents, and moved at their blindness, and by the impulse of the Holy Ghost, he spoke to them of our faith, and even promised them posterity if they consented to receive baptism. The grace which accompanied his words enlightened their understanding, and triumphed over their will; they became Christians, and obtained the long-desired happiness that Publius had promised them as the reward of their conversion. At the moment of my birth they gave me the name of Lumena, in allusion to the light of faith, of which I had been, as it were, the fruit; and the day of my baptism they called me Filumena, or daughter of light (filia luminis) because on that day I was born to the faith. *

Don Francis observes that in giving, in the first edition of his work, this etymology to the name of Philomena, he himself hesitated to admit it, but that an interior impulse continually urged him, in spite of his repugnance, not only to write it then, but to repeat it again in the following editions. It appeared, indeed, more natural to take the root of this word from the Greek language, which gives a different sense, although analogous to the first, and it is that of well-beloved as the saint is, in fact, particularly so.

The affection which my parents bore me was so great that they would have me always with them. It was on this account that they carried me with them to Rome, in a journey that my father was obliged to make on the occasion of an unjust war with which he was threatened by the haughty Diocletian. I was then thirteen years old. Being arrived in the capital of the world, we three proceeded to the palace of the emperor, and were admitted to an audience. As soon as Diocletian saw me his eyes were fixed upon me; he appeared to be prepossessed in this manner during the entire time that my father was stating with animated feelings everything that could serve for his defense. As soon as he had ceased to speak, the emperor desired him to be no longer disturbed, but that, banishing all fear, he should think only of living in happiness. 'I shall place at your disposal all the force of the empire, and shall ask in return only one thing -- that is, the hand of your daughter.' My father, dazzled with an honor he was far from expecting, willingly acceded on the spot to the proposal of the emperor, and when we had returned to our own dwelling, my father and mother did all they could to induce me to yield to Diocletian's wishes, and to theirs. What! said I to them, do you wish that for the love of a man I should break the promise I made two years since to Jesus Christ? My virginity belongs to Him, I can no longer dispose of it.' 'But you were then too young,' answered my father, 'to form such an engagement,' and he joined the most terrible threats to the command that he gave me to accept the hand of Diocletian. The grace of my God rendered me invincible, and my father, not being able to make the emperor allow of the reasons he alleged, in order to disengage himself from the promise he had given, was obliged, by his order, to bring me into his presence.

"I had to withstand for some moments beforehand a new attack from my father's anger and affection. My mother, uniting her efforts to his, endeavored to conquer my resolution. Caresses, threats, everything was employed to reduce me to compliance. At last I saw both of them fall at my knees, and say to me with tears in their eyes, 'My child, have pity on thy father, thy mother, thy country, our subjects.' No, no, I answered them: God, and that virginity which I have vowed to Him, before everything; before you, before my country! My kingdom is heaven. My words plunged them into despair, and they brought me before the emperor, who, on his part, did all in his power to win me; but his promises, his allurements, his threats, were equally useless. He then got into a violent fit of anger, and, influenced by the devil, he had me cast into one of the prisons of his palace, where I was forthwith loaded with chains. Thinking that pain and shame would weaken the courage that my divine Spouse inspired me with, he came to see me every day; and then, after having my chains loosed, that I might take the small portion of bread and water which I received as food, he renewed his attacks, some of which, if not for the grace of God, would have been fatal to purity. The defeats which he always experienced were for me the preludes to new tortures; but prayer supported me; I ceased not to recommend myself to Jesus, and His most pure Mother. My captivity had lasted thirty-seven days, when, in the midst of a heavenly light, I saw Mary holding her divine Son in her arms. 'My daughter.' said she to me, 'three days more of prison, and, after forty days, thou shalt leave this state of pain.' Such happy news made my heart beat with joy, but as the Queen of angels had added that I should quit my prison to sustain, in frightful torments, a combat far more terrible than those preceding, I passed instantly from joy to the most cruel anguish; I thought it would kill me. 'Have courage, my child,' said Mary then to me: 'art thou unaware of the love of predilection that I bear to thee? The name which thou receivedst in baptism is the pledge of it, by the resemblance which it has to that of my Son and to mine. Thou art called Lumena, as thy Spouse is called Light, Star, Sun; as I myself am called Aurora, Star, the Moon in the fullness of its brightness, and Sun. Fear not, I will aid thee. Now nature, whose weakness humbles thee, asserts its law; in the moment of combat, grace will come to lend thee its force, and thy angel, who was also mine, Gabriel, whose name expresses force, will come to thy succor: I will recommend thee especially to his care, as the well-beloved among my children.' These words of the Queen of virgins gave me again courage, and the vision disappeared, leaving my prison filled with a celestial perfume.

"What she had announced to me was soon realized. Diocletian, despairing of bending me, took the resolution of having me publicly tortured, and the first torment to which he condemned me was to be scourged. 'Since she is not ashamed,' said he, 'to prefer, to an emperor like me, a malefactor, condemned by his own nation to an infamous death, she deserves that my justice shall treat her as he was treated.' He then ordered my clothes to be taken off, and that I should be tied to a column; and, in the presence of a great number of gentlemen of his court, he had me beaten with such violence, that my body, bathed in blood, appeared but one single wound. The tyrant, perceiving that I was going to faint and die, had me removed from his eyes, and dragged again to prison, where he believed I would breathe out my last sigh. But he was disappointed, as I was also in the delightful hope of going quickly to rejoin my Spouse; for two angels, shining with light, appeared to me, and pouring a health-giving balm upon my wounds, rendered me more vigorous than I had been before the torture. The next morning the emperor was informed of it; he had me brought into his presence, viewed me with astonishment, and then sought to persuade me that I owed my cure to the Jupiter whom he adored. 'He desires positively,' said he, 'that you should be empress of Rome.' And, joining to these seductive words promises of the greatest honors, and the most flattering caresses, he endeavored to complete the work of hell which he had begun; but the divine Spirit, to whom I am indebted for my constancy, filled me at the moment with so much light and knowledge, that to all the proofs which I gave of the solidity of our faith, neither Diocletian nor any of his courtiers could give any answer whatever. Then his frenzy came on anew, and he commanded me to be buried, with an anchor to my neck, in the waters of the Tiber. The order was executed, but God permitted that it should not succeed; for, at the moment in which I was precipitated into the river, two angels came again to my succor, and, after having cut the rope that bound me to the anchor, while the anchor fell to the bottom of the Tiber, where it has remained till the present time, they transported me gently, in the view of an immense multitude, upon the banks, of the river. This miracle worked happy effects upon a great number of spectators, and they were converted to the faith; but Diocletian, attributing it to secret magic, had me dragged through the streets of Rome, and then ordered that I should be shot in a shower of arrows. I was stuck all over with them; my blood flowed on all sides; when he commanded me, exhausted and dying, to be carried back to my dungeon. Heaven honored me with a new favor there. I fell into a sweet sleep, and I found myself, on awaking, perfectly cured. Diocletian learns it. 'Well, then,' he cried, in a fit of rage, 'let her be pierced with sharp darts a second time, and let her die in that torture.' They hastened to obey him. The archers bent their bows, they gathered all their strength; but the arrows refused to second their intentions. The emperor was present; he became enraged at the sight; he called me a magician, and, thinking that the action of fire could destroy the enchantment, he ordered the darts to be made red in a furnace, and directed a second time against me. It was done, indeed; but these darts, after having gone over a part of the space which they were to cross to come to me, took quite a contrary direction, and returned to strike those by whom they had been hurled. Six of the archers were killed by them, and several among them renounced paganism, and the people began to render public testimony to the power of the God that had protected me. These murmurs and acclamations made the tyrant fear some more painful accident; he therefore hastened to terminate my days, by ordering my head to be cut off. Thus did my soul take flight toward my heavenly Spouse, who placed me, with the crown of virginity and the palm of martyrdom, in a distinguished rank among the elect, who partake of the enjoyment of his divine presence. The day that was so happy for me, and saw me enter into glory, was a Friday, and the hour of my death was the third after mid-day (that is to say, the same hour that saw my divine Master expire)."

Such is, according to this revelation, the history of the martyrdom of St. Philomena. The reader sees in it nothing but what is pious, holy, and edifying; he finds in it, also, proofs above suspicion of the truth of the facts which it contains. He will, perhaps, say to himself, in thinking of the numerous and brilliant miracles, which have rendered the name of the holy martyr so celebrated in the world, that it was becoming that the Lord should manifest, at least partially, her merits. The faithful, by this means, are more edified, and the glory of God, as well as virtue, which He honors in St. Philomena, is promoted in a great degree. But since it has not pleased the divine wisdom to leave, in the historical monuments, any trace of so great generosity and such heroism, by what other means than that of revelation could the knowledge of them come to our age? To our age!

This expression includes many reflections. It is the age of pride, it is the age of incredulity, the age in which they desire to subject to the false lights of a wandering reason the very thoughts and conduct of God. For this age, the divine wisdom of Providence, so admirable in the variety of its combinations, is but folly, a jest; it turns into ridicule the enlightened simplicity of faith; it treats everything of a supernatural order as superstition and fable; it jests at belief, it despises holiness, it devotes to its hatred those whom God has charged with its instruction. The light, nevertheless, destined to enlighten the world, ceases not to shine. If those ungrateful beings are unwilling to profit by it, let them shut their eyes -- that is in their power; although, to say the truth, if they kept them open to fix them upon the works of God, their countenance should blush in beholding what His power operates, and what instruments He uses to display it. A woman! An unknown virgin! All kinds of wonders wrought through her invocation; wrought in favor of those whom the world persecutes! Performed in the bosom of the Roman Church, whose practices are thus rendered more estimable, its sacraments more frequented, its ministers more venerable, its name, faith, and doctrine more clear to its children. What a humiliation for them! And this is the fruit of the world's secret practices, its infamous writings, which are become almost as numerous as the sands of the sea. I think I see Goliath, struck again by the stone from the brook, roll expiring at the feet of David, who cuts off his head. Or rather, the proud Holofernes, killed in his drunkenness by the weak hand of a woman: and, while Nabuchodonosor, the image of Satan, as his general is the image of the vile multitude which Satan directs, grows pale and shakes upon his throne, at the news of the check which his invincible army has received, the faithful, figured by the Jews of Bethulia, make the skies ring with their shouts of thanksgiving and of victory, and bless with emulation the new Judith, whose powerful arm has saved them. God could not choose, in His infinite treasures, a means more suited than this to confound the pride of the age, and to give triumph to His cause.

Chapter III. Translation of the relics of St. Philomena to Mugnano, and the miracles that followed.

It has been observed that the body of our saint had remained in obscurity at Rome in the year 1805. Divine Providence was pleased to draw it from that state, and to glorify it in the following manner : --

Don Francis de Lucia, a zealous and holy missionary of Italy, came from Naples to Rome with Don Bartholomew of Cesarea, who was chosen by the Holy See to govern the diocese of Potenza. He felt an anxious desire to obtain for his domestic chapel the body of a saint of a known name,* and the Bishop of Potenza having seconded him in the steps he took for this purpose, he was introduced, shortly after his arrival, into the apartment where they have collected those blessed remains, in order that he might himself make his selection.

* The ancient Christians, when so fortunate as to obtain possession of the mangled remains of the martyrs, frequently buried them without distinguishing their graves by the empty honor of a name. This apparent neglect may have arisen from the same cause that leaves so many graves in our burial-grounds unmarked by a stone. Besides, it often happened that criminals, amongst whom Christians were classed, were sent from the remote provinces of the empire, that their deaths might afford a sight for

that heartless generation. Indeed, so little did the Christians esteem the remembrance of the world they despised, that in Martyr of Christ was comprised all their desire, their glory, and their hope: hence, in the catacombs, the place selected for their burial, such inscriptions as the following have been found : --

MARCELLA ET CHRISTI MARTYRES CCCCCL. (Marcella and 550 Martyrs of Christ.) HIC REQUIESCIT MEDICUS CUM PLURIBUS.

(Here rests Medicus with many.) CL MARTYRES CHRISTI. (150 Martyrs of Christ.)

When he came into the presence of the bones of the holy martyr, he felt, as he tells himself, a sudden and quite extraordinary joy, which, showing itself at the same time upon his countenance, was remarked with surprise by Monsignor Ponzetti, keeper of the sacred relics. All his wishes, from that moment, were for these sacred bones, which he preferred to all the others, without being able to explain the motive. He did not venture, however, to manifest his choice, fearing a refusal, when he was told, on the part of the keeper, that he, having observed his predilection for St. Philomena, was willing to grant her to him; and the person added these remarkable words: -- " Monsignor is persuaded that the saint wishes to go to your country, where she will work great miracles."

This news filled the soul of the good missionary with consolation, and he only thought of the means of transferring the holy remains. They were to be delivered to him that very day; but as that day, and the two other following days, passed without seeing the promise fulfilled, he began to fear lest the keeper would recall his intention. It was, indeed, a thing unusual at Rome, to give to a private person an entire saint's body, and above all, with a proper name, because at that time the annual excavations produced very few of this kind, and for this reason they were only given to bishops or churches. Monsignor Ponzetti then informed Don Francis that it was impossible for him to accede to his wishes, and he offered him his choice among the twelve bodies without names.

Don Francis found himself, at this intimation, in a great embarrassment, as well on account of the preparations he had made, the letters he had written on the subject to Mugnano, and other circumstances unnecessary to be here mentioned, as also from the anxiety with which he felt himself oppressed when he attempted to fix his choice upon another saint. How admirable is the providence of God m the secrecy of its ways! These difficulties, and many others also, were only to make known more clearly the divine will in regard of the destination of this blessed body, and to glorify it the more; for shortly after, without the missionary daring even to think of it, he became, first, the depository, and then the master of it.

The persons charged with translating the sacred relics of St. Philomena to Mugnano, set out from Naples toward the evening. They had counted upon the light of the moon to guide them during the night, and, therefore, did not provide any other means for lighting their way, in case of need. Thus, when a darkness covered the sky, which threatened to deluge them with rain, they had no protection to recur to but that of the saint: and God was pleased, for the glory of His servant, that it should not be sought in vain; for while the pious escort invoked her with fervor, a column of light was suddenly formed in the air, the lower part of which rested upon the shrine, where it remained steadily fixed until daylight, while the upper part of it reached up to the sky, and showed a certain number of stars, that appeared to form about it a belt.

The octave day of the translation, during the solemn Mass, in presence of the crowd which assisted at it, a child, about ten years old, stood up in the middle of the church, and walked over to the shrine to thank her benefactress. Her mother, a poor widow, had carried her in her arms into the church, and from the beginning of the Mass until the elevation, the moment of the miracle, had unceasingly and fervently supplicated the saint. She joined her voice to those who glorified God for having conferred such power on St. Philomena. The child cured had been a cripple; it could neither walk nor stand; it was known to all the village, and all the village after Mass saw it walk through the streets, announcing the miracle of which it had been the object, and to which they all bore testimony, both in congratulating the child, and in filling the air with their joyful acclamations.

The miracle wrought during the holy sacrifice attracted such a concourse to vespers, that the church could not hold all the people: a great number remained outside, among whom was a woman of the village of Avella, holding in her arms a little girl, about two years old, who had been blinded by the small-pox. The most celebrated physicians of the capital had been consulted; they considered the disease incurable. But the afflicted mother, knowing that the things impossible to man are possible with God, did not despair of the cure of her daughter; she ran to Mugnano, and although the passage to the saint appeared to be stopped, for the reason above mentioned, she succeeded in making her way to the shrine. Animated, immediately, with a living faith, she takes some oil from the lamp that burned before St. Philomena; she anointed with it the eyes of her child, and the little incurable was instantly cured. At this miracle there are new cries of joy, and new emotions produced by exultation and gratitude. The people outside the church re-echo the acclamations from within. The preacher (for all this took place during the sermon), Don Antonio Verano, could no longer be heard; and as everyone was demanding with clamor to see the child that had been cured, a priest took it in his arms, and mounting upon a balustrade, he presented it to the view of the people, who, filled with wonder, proclaimed aloud the power of God and the glory of His servant.

There took place, during the following days, a great number of similar miracles, the accounts of which have been published. We shall now say a word on the erection of their chapel to the saint.

The first intention of Don Francis was to leave the relics in the church of our Lady delle Grazie, He destined them, as we said, for his private oratory. The numerous miracles, however, worked since their arrival at Mugnano, showed him that such was not the design of the Most High. He resigned himself, therefore, willingly to the sacrifice which Divine Providence required of him, and occupied himself henceforward only with the thought of erecting, in that same church, an altar, where the saint might receive the homage of the devout. This altar was shortly after erected. It was placed in one of the chapels of the church; but its simplicity corresponded little with the celebrity of the holy martyr, and the grandeur of the miracles with which the Lord had been pleased to honor her. It is not meant to make any reproach to the people of Mugnano; they were poor, as well as the most part of those among whom the saint shared her favors. Their alms, which were abundant, considering their

moderate means, were scarcely sufficient, particularly during the troubles of Italy, for the maintenance of the public worship of the saint. They could, therefore, only form the desire of seeing the saint's sanctuary adorned in a more suitable manner. God was pleased to second their pious wishes; and for this end, He made use of one of those circumstances which are regarded by men as ordinary, but which, in the mind of God, are designed to manifest His glory and to honor His saints.

A celebrated advocate of Naples, by name Alexander Serio, had, for a long time, a great devotion toward St. Philomena, and his wife united with him in this devotion. As they had considerable estates in the territory of Mugnano, they came there in 1814, exactly at that time when each year they celebrated the feast of the Translation. Don Serio had been suffering for several years from an internal disease, which was wasting him away. His wife, though deeply afflicted, was still full of hope in the mediation of St. Philomena; she prayed to her, and got others to offer fervent prayers to obtain the recovery of her husband. The day of the fete on which occasion she redoubled her entreaties, together with her confidence, when she was about to conclude, after the benediction of the most blessed Sacrament had been given, Don Alexander, who was in the church with his wife, was attacked with violent pains in his bowels, which seemed to threaten his life. He was quickly carried home, and his disease, in a few hours, made such a rapid and alarming progress, that his life was despaired of. He was unable even to confess himself. His poor wife, overpowered with grief, exclaimed, in her deep affliction: "Is this, then, O St. Philomena, the favor you have obtained for me?" and immediately, by an inspiration of faith, laying hold of an image of the saint, she threw it on her dying husband, asking, at least, the favor of seeing him comforted by the last sacraments before he should expire. With this prayer she made a vow: she promised, in the name of her husband, to have erected in the chapel of St. Philomena an altar of marble. At that moment the dying man recovered the use of his senses. He declared he was out of danger, confessed himself in an edifying manner, and as soon as he had finished his confession, he no longer felt pain and the usual symptoms of the malady that so long afflicted him had disappeared.

The favor being granted, the promise was fulfilled; they went even beyond their engagement; thenceforward, the sanctuary, now so celebrated, presented to the crowd of pilgrims that visited it a more consoling sight for their devotion. There was one thing which particularly attracted their attention, namely, the great marble slab that covered the altar, and on which were still visible the marks of a miracle. The workman, in using his chisel to fit it into its place, split it nearly the whole of its breadth. A number of persons were present, and it may be imagined what trouble was felt by them and what confusion by the workman. He was, notwithstanding this accident, very expert in his art; and feeling humbled by this awkwardness, he set himself to mend the breach. The breach was at the beginning more than a finger wide; he endeavored to unite the edges by means of a plate of iron, and then filled the opening with cement. The finger of the saint aiding the hand of the workman, by a wonderful miracle, joined in its former state the marble that had been separated in so remarkable a manner. She left merely at the place where it had been split a line of a deep color, which might be taken for a vein in tile stone by a person unacquainted with the miracle.

In 1831, there was at Naples a poor washer-woman, whose state of pregnancy caused her much suffering. The name of this poor woman was Anne Moccia, and her husband's, Joseph Cagiano. To obtain some ease in her sufferings, she resolved to burn, day and night, a lamp before the image of the saint, and this resolution she kept strictly, as long as her means enabled her. But one evening, as she found herself without oil or money, she thus with simplicity addressed the saint: "My dear saint, I have nothing for you or for me; here we are both in the dark; but as I must go to work, let me leave you and say good-by." After locking her own and taking the key, she went away to the next House, that she might work by the light of her neighbor's lamp. The night was far advanced when she returned home. She opened her door, and to her great astonishment found the lamp lighting and filled with oil, and her humble dwelling miraculously illuminated. She ran instantly to the window, called her neighbors, and told what had happened, and invited them to return thanks to St. Philomena for this feeling act of her goodness, which was the forerunner of several others. The good woman, however, appeared not to be better than before, and her time being come, she had to endure, during five days, violent pains, which seemed to endanger her life. The midwife was certain that the infant was dead for three days past. The illness increased every moment. The poor patient got brought to her the image of the saint, and taking it in her hand, she spoke to her in this manner: "Is this, then, what I have asked of you? is this the return for the oil I have expended?" Whilst she was venting herself in mild complaint, an infant was born, but it was dead. The midwife, who expected as much, had sufficient address to conceal the fact from the mother, and while she bestowed on her all her care, the little creature remained on the floor, without even being wrapped up, and this in a very cold season -- it was the 13th of March. An hour and a half had already passed, when the poor mother became aware of her misfortune. In the bitterness of her grief she was heard to utter these words: "A great favor you have indeed done me! Away! I don't wish you any longer in my house. Take this image; put it out of my sight." Such expressions may perhaps shock one, but the living faith that prompted them moved Heaven, and was repaid by a mighty favor; for at that same moment the infant moved; it cried, and everyone in the house ran toward it, shouting out, "A miracle! a miracle!" It was baptized, and after thirty-five days its innocent soul departed, to join in heaven her who obtained for it the two-fold life of nature and of grace. This miracle made a great noise at Naples; and several learned and pious ecclesiastics published it in all directions to the honor of the glorious saint.

Chapter IV. Miracles wrought in favor of children.

Rose de Lucia, cousin of Don Francis, had a child about eight years old, which, in spite of the mother's care and all the efforts of medicine, had been sinking under a severe sickness: at last he expired in the sight of his parents and of several other

persons. His poor mother could scarcely believe her dear child was no more. She tried every means to justify a hope that her heart could not quit; but, finally, everything proving unavailing, she became aware of the afflicting certainty that her son was dead; St. Philomena had not heard the ardent prayers that had been so often addressed to her by a disconsolate mother. In the bitterness of her heart, her faith seemed to revive with increased force. She ran to the image of the saint, took it from the wall to which it was hung, and threw it upon the lifeless body of her child, asking, with loud cries and torrents of tears, that her son might be restored. At that moment the corpse arose, and, as if he had awakened from sleep, he moved to the foot of his bed; and those eyes that had already wept him dead, beheld him, not only returned to life without the least symptom of illness, but vigorous and full of health.

At Monteforte a miracle not less extraordinary took place. One Lelio Gesualdo, and his wife, Antonia Valentino, had a little daughter named Rosa Fortunata, at the time eleven months old: she was their only and dearly loved child. One day, somehow or other, this infant escaped from the hands of the person who carried it, and fell from a window into the street. The height of the window was eighty palms (sixty feet). The fall must have been rapid, for the head of the child striking against a brick chimney, detached from it several splinters, and then fell upon the pavement. Its mother, who witnessed this dreadful accident, cried out, "Good St. Philomena, this child belongs to you if you save her for me!" The father of the little Rosa, who was in the street at the same time, made, in his fright, the same exclamation, and ran to the child, which lay stretched upon the ground; he took it up, and saw neither wound nor bruise, and there was on its person no other mark of the fall, than the breaking of a silver ornament that was about its neck.

Another child, about eleven years old, of the name of Giacomo d'Elia, son of a surgeon of Visciano, had his foot broken by the wheel of a carriage that passed over it. The pain was so great that he became insensible, and was carried home half dead. Immediately, not-withstanding the efforts of art, the wound became gangrenous, and, on account of the extreme weakness of the boy, amputation being impracticable, his death was daily expected. In this state of things a priest of the place arrived; he had an image of the saint, and exposed it to the veneration of the family, and recommended them to interest St. Philomena in their favor. They knelt down and recited in common the litany of the Blessed Virgin, and the priest, approaching the bed of the child, awoke him from his lethargy, and showed him the image of the saint. At the sight, young d'Elia began to speak, and appeared to be no longer ill: the wound was quickly uncovered, when it was seen that the gangrene had disappeared; the foot was cured, the child got up, and, although he wanted a toe, he walked with perfect ease.

The favor that had been obtained by a child not five years old was not less extraordinary. This favor might be attributed to the name she bore. She was called Philomena, and the saint has always marked a particular affection for the children who have received this name in baptism. The parents of Philomena were Maria Monteforte and Kicolo Canonico. One day, as the child was playing near an oven, the door came off and fell upon her foot, and end off the fourth toe. At the cries of the child they hastened to her relief; they laid her on her bed, and after examining the hurt, which might become serious, they called a surgeon, who applied the remedies that his art suggests. Night came, and the little Philomena could not sleep; but, as she herself related, and the result proved the truth of her account, while the whole family were sleeping, the saint appeared to her, gave her some sweet-meats, saying, "My little Philomena, take courage! You will tell your mamma that she must weep no more, and that I will cure you." She disappeared. The child began immediately to cry out, calling its mother; the mother ran to the child, as well as all the persons in the house. Philomena told them in her own way what she had seen, what had been given her, and what she had been commanded to communicate to her mother. This announcement filled the family with gratitude and joy. They long to see the cure take place. They saw it realized the next morning; for she walked about as before, but still wanted the toe that had been cut off. It was hoped that the saint would finish the work she had begun, when they heard that Philomena had received a second and a third visit, and that caressing her little protege the saint had each time bestowed on her some sweet thing. This hope was not vain. Two days before the feast of the saint, Philomena received a toe in place of the one she had lost. But it was not the same as the former one, which had been buried in the church-yard, but another, proportioned to the rest of the foot, which it was easy to see was there by some extraordinary operation.

There was another Philomena somewhat older than the preceding, and perhaps also more giddy. Her parents' names were Tommaso Tedeseo and Ursula Serio. This event happened in 1830. The day of St. Philomena's feast she was amusing herself by cutting with a pair of scissors, when, by some awkwardness, she drove them into her right eye; during five days there issued from the wound blood and water. The afflicted family had recourse to the intercession of the holy martyr, but imprudently saying that they would rather see her dead than blind. Don Francis, informed of the accident and of the inconsiderate prayers of the family, goes to them, and after reproaching them a little, he calls the child, and says to her, "My dear, go directly to the church; put your finger into the lamp of the saint, and with the oil that will be on the finger, carefully, yourself, anoint the wound." Philomena obeys, and does exactly as she had been desired. The faith of the child obtained her a miraculous favor: the eye was perfectly cured, contrary to the expectation of the doctors, who had pronounced it incurable; and besides this, there was observed something more brilliant in it than in the left eye. Philomena gathered a still more precious fruit from this prodigy. Her faith was so singularly increased, that it merited to be rewarded by another favor equally wonderful. Some days afterward she met one of her cousins whose face had been severely burned by the fire-works on the day of a fete. She immediately set about persuading him to imitate her example. According to her, nothing was more easy than to be cured; it was only necessary to go and take some oil, and to rub with it the eye and cheek, and all would be done. The little boy is convinced; he goes, and does as his cousin told him, and the next day in waking he found himself so perfectly cured, that in seeing him, one would have doubted if anything had happened to him. Here I would be tempted to exclaim with our divine Master, "I confess to thee, O Father, Lord of heaven and earth, because thou hast hid these things from the wise and prudent, and hast revealed them to little ones." -- (Matt, xi. 25.) But what is this mystery? Have we not all received faith, of which so few, so few, indeed, amongst Christians, know how to make available the inexhaustible resources!

The poor have also an abundant share in the favors of St. Philomena. At Vista, a town situated at the foot of Mount Gargano, there lived a very virtuous, but miserably poor family. The extreme poverty in which they were in the country, obliged them to come to town in order to see if they could gain there a trifle to enable them to subsist. The husband's name was Giovanni Troya, and his wife's Maria Teresa Bovini. A ruined cabin, around which was a small garden, formed all their property and all their hopes. In this afflicting situation, the view of the future afforded little consolation; Maria Teresa, particularly, seeing herself on the eve of giving an infant to the world, could not think on this subject without feeling her heart oppressed with grief. "Where can she place her child? How shall she procure for it the requisite clothes?" But God can do all things, and St. Philomena, if she wishes to aid me, can work a miracle for me." In this manner she encouraged herself to bear her affliction, and often she prayed to the saint not to abandon her in her distress. At last the dreaded hour came, and the earnestly-sought relief did not yet appear. The embarrassment both of the mother and the person who assisted her was exceedingly great. Maria Teresa made her complaint to the saint. The woman sought everywhere for a bit of linen to cover the child, for the destitution of this family was such that even a miserable rag was not to be found. Moved with compassion, the woman took a handkerchief from her shoulders and wrapped the child in it, and the afflicted mother, seeing that there was wanting a band to swathe the child, said she had one, though half torn and much worn, in a trunk which she showed. The woman ran and opened it, but what was her surprise when she saw there a little bundle of neat and elegant clothes, arranged with order! There issued from them so sweet an odor, that the air was embalmed with it. She took the treasure and kissed it; the mother, overpowered with joy, did the same, and was imable to express her gratitude to her heavenly benefactress. The infant, thus richly dressed, was carried to the baptismal font. The news of the miracle spread abroad, and persons came from all quarters to kiss the wonderful clothes, and to breathe the heavenly perfume they exhaled. The saint did not stop here. The next night Maria Teresa was awakened by the cries of the little child; and by the light of a dim lamp that lighted the room, she sought for the child, which she did not find in the place she had laid it. Doubting and in fear, she turned to another side, where she beheld a young person dressed in white, and of a heavenly beauty; who held in her arms the little child, which she was affectionately caressing. "What a consolation for the poor mother! Seized with respect, joy, confusion, and gratitude, she cannot help exclaiming, "Ah, St. Philomena!" And St. Philomena kissed the child and laid it again in its place, and disappeared. Maria Teresa was, during several days, in a kind of ecstasy from the effect of this sight; and we who read this, ought we to restrain our admiration and joy? Ah! blessed are the simple souls, and the hearts truly faithful! Blessed is innocence and poverty, rich in faith! At the celebration of the feast of St. Philomena, in 1830, the magnificence was great and the concourse extraordinary. All the bells were in motion; and as children are often fond of going into places where prudence does not guide them, it happened that a little boy mounted up to one of the steeples, from which he fell down on the pavement. The height of the place from which he fell was about fifty palms. His companions thought he was killed; they uttered a shout; the people ran, and, while expecting to see him dashed to pieces and lifeless, they saw him, full of vigor, get up and run, and, proud of his fall, mount up again to the belfry from which he had just tumbled down. He owed, he said, his preservation to the name of St. Philomena, for at the moment of his fall he had invoked her.

On the eve of the same day, a similar miracle took place. A child, nine years old, while standing upon a high rock, fell, in the presence of its parents, into a deep valley which the rock overhung. Her parents ran to her succor, and, when they lifted her up, they found she was insensible and apparently lifeless. Pierced with the keenest grief, they threw themselves on their knees, and loudly called on their blessed protectress, saying, "Blessed Philomena, good Saint Philomena, do not let us bring our child back dead to the home from which we have brought her full of life! Oh! come, we beseech you, to our relief." And, in their affliction, to move the heart of the saint, as a mortification, practiced in that country, they began to rub their tongues to the rocks, saying they would not cease till their prayer was granted. The child, however, did not come to herself; the appearances were more alarming; in seeing her and touching her you would have supposed her dead. The poor parents did not lose confidence, they cried again to heaven, they imposed on themselves new mortifications, and at length they had reason to be proud of their faith and perseverance. The little girl awoke as if from a deep sleep; she called her parents, and, while they were running to her, she got up and went to meet them. They sought in vain for any mark on her body, she felt nothing ailed her, the saint had repaired all in the twinkling of an eye, and the family went on foot to thank her for the benefit which they owed to her powerful intercession.

Chapter V. Favors granted through the intercession of St. Philomena.

One morning, as Don Francis was entering the church to say mass, he saw his mother run toward him, saying, with an affrighted look, "Give me a moment; I have something to tell you; I feel myself strongly urged to tell it to you." He desires her to speak ; and she began to recount a vision or dream which she had had on the preceding night. "I saw," said she, "St. Philomena preparing for a journey; and, fearing that she wished to leave us, I was weeping, with many of the inhabitants of Mugnano, and begged of her to remain with us. She then, with the kindest accent, encouraged us, telling us she would return the next day; but that the family of Terres, to whom she owed many obligations, being exposed to great peril, gratitude required that she should go to protect them from it." Don Francis regarded this dream as the effect of the imagination; he could not help, however, after a little reflection, writing

on the subject to tlie family of Terres. They received his letter, opened it, and were astonished to find in it an event which had like to have destroyed them the night before. Robbers, disguised as foreign soldiers, whose language they borrowed, had come to get lodging, as they said. As the door was not opened for them, they began to force it; they threatened fire and sword; and massacre was about to commence, when an incident, ordered by Heaven, came to baffle their sanguinary intentions. The Terres had no sooner seen themselves in danger, than all the family implored the succor of St. Philomena, "No," said they, " the saint will not abandon us; let us pray, let us have confidence in her; we shall be delivered from this danger." Their hope was not in vain. At the moment that the assassins were rushing toward the staircase, after having forced in the door, the family heard several voices, which were well known, call from without, "Light, light! Quick, quick! bring us light!" And these cries, several times repeated, reaching the ears of the robbers, as well as of the people of the house, encouraged the latter, and scared the former, and in the twinkling of an eye the danger was over. The robbers having taken flight, the Terres saw their friends come in, both to their joy and the others' surprise. The different circumstances of this event appeared to both parties very singular; but, on the next morning, when the letter arrived, the mystery was explained. The family of Terres, and their neighbors, who, without knowing why, had come to visit so late, discovered in what had passed the finger of the saint, and thanked her in all the effusion of their hearts.

St. Philomena comes, not only invisibly, but visibly, to the succor of those who invoke her. A wood-cutter of Sirignano, called Carluccio Napolitano, favored, on account of his devotion toward the saint, with several graces, had a great confidence in her. This worthy man carried always about him one of her portraits, before which he used to open his heart, in his various necessities. One time, as he was journeying, being surprised by the night, he went into an inn. The conversation turned on St. Philomena, and he produced his portrait of her, to show it to the persons present; it pleased one of them, and he offered two pieces of money for it, another offered three, then four, five, and even twelve. But Carluccio answered that he would not give it for a Roman crown, and that it was too good company for him, and then he replaced it in his pocket-book. The next morning he got up very early, and directed his steps toward a village, called the Sorbo, where he had to work. In crossing a thick forest, he went astray, and soon, not knowing either where he was, or where he was going, his heart turned to his good saint, to whom he thus spoke: "My dear saint, yesterday I would not part with you, even for a good sum of money; I preferred your company to everything, and today you see me astray in this wood, and you don't come to my relief!" He had not finished these words, when he saw coming a young person, of about thirteen years of age, dressed in a robe of sky blue, and of great beauty and modesty. She looks at him, and says to him, "My good man, what is the matter with you? what trouble has happened to you?" Carluccio explains his embarrassment. "That is nothing," she replies; "follow me, and I will set you again on your road." And, without saying more, she went forward, as if to show him the way. "Walking after her, a little surprised at the circumstance, he said to himself, "Now, it may be seen what great goodness St. Philomena has! She runs to assist one, when one has scarcely called her; for I cannot doubt but that it is she that has sent to me this amiable little child." He was occupying himself with these pions thoughts, when the

young girl stopped, and, turning toward him, said, "Follow, now, that road, for near a mile; you will then meet a woman with a basket on her head; she is going to the place you seek. You will go along with her, and shortly after you will arrive at the place." Carluccio thanked her affectionately, and they separated. He turned round to see where the charitable lady was going, but he could see her no longer, and he continued his way, without further reflection. Immediately afterward he found himself in a new difficulty. The path along which he went terminated in several others, and which to choose he knew not; lifting up his eyes, he saw at the same time advancing toward him the woman he had been told of; he recognized her by the basket. "Do you know," he instantly said to her, "which of these paths leads to the village of Sorbo?" " Sorbo!" replies the villager, "I know the way; it is my village; come and I will bring you to it." And he reached the village shortly after. It was then that the eyes of Carluccio were opened. How could this young lady, so genteel, so modest, so elegantly dressed, be traveling in the wood? How could she have guessed his embarrassment, and answered his thought?

How could she foresee what was to happen to him, and to represent to him so accurately the woman, the load she was carrying, and the place where she was going? "No, no," said he to himself, "it has not been chance; it is St. Philomena herself that I have seen, and who has extricated me from the difficulty I was in." During several days, Carluccio seemed almost beside himself; his heart was filled with a particular love and devotion toward his celestial guide.

The special court of Avellino, the sentences of which are without appeal, had condemned to death a man named Pellegrino Ruocco, together with two other criminals. The sentence being intimated to the condemned, preparing them for death was the only occupation of the persons about them. The next day, the 19th of August, 1832, the sentence was to take effect. Pellegrino had in the town an aunt, who bore him a great affection. The mournful news soon reached her, and, almost as soon, she, together with some other pious persons, fled to the church, where they offered up fervent prayers for her unhappy nephew. A three-days' devotion was, at the time, celebrating in honor of the blessed martyr. After having implored the succor of the Queen of Virgins, these women, full of faith, went to the altar of St. Philomena, and asked her, with lamentations mingled with tears, to vouchsafe to interest herself in obtaining the pardon of the condemned man. The crowd that was in the church paying their homage to the saint, could not refrain, on hearing them, from disapproving of their conduct. " Why," said they, " ask the pardon of a criminal after the sentence has been passed? Would it not have been better to have prayed beforehand? And what way is there to obtain the pardon?" It was in this manner the people reasoned; the good aunt thought differently. Persuaded that to the Lord and his saints nothing is impossible, she returned home, and, prostrate before an image of St. Philomena, she persevered in asking the pardon of her nephew. She thought she heard then an interior voice, which said to her distinctly, "Go, set out for Naples; cast yourself at the feet of the king, and the pardon will be granted to you." As she did not know whence this advice could come, she continued her prayer: the more she prayed, the more she heard the voice; but when she began to see something supernatural in it, a difficulty started: it appeared to her that she could never succeed in such an enterprise. However, tlie divine light cleared it up; she decided on the journey; she set out from Avellino, toward six and three-quarters of the same day, and, after having run thirty miles, she arrived in the capital toward midnight. That same night, her nephew, who had no knowledge of the project of his aunt, recommended himself ardently to the blessed martyr; and, having fallen into a slumber, he thought he saw her, and heard her utter these words: "Fear not; be content: though you should be at the gibbet, I will know how to rescue you from the hands of your executioners." He awoke, and at the moment he communicated the favorable dream to his companions. The next day he told it to the persons that came to see him; the joy that animated, at the moment, his countenance, revealed what was passing in his heart; he was unshaken in his confidence. His aunt was, however, in a great embarrassment. The petition was ready, and the liberty of an audience obtained; but the king would not be visible until about two o'clock in the afternoon, and the sentence was to be executed at Avellino, at five o'clock, the same day. 'No matter; God can do everything. Already, against all human expectation, the pardon is obtained.

Legal forms are to be filled up; but if a miracle is requisite to have it arrive before the execution, St. Philomena is at hand to work it. It is impossible not to remark here the attention of God to exalt the glory of his servant. He permitted new and almost insurmountable difficulties to arise; for, in place of expediting at once the pardon, full two hours were suffered to elapse, and four o'clock struck (there remained, then, but one hour before the time when the execution should take place), when the king recollected the pardon, and that it had not been dispatched. A new obstacle arose; he had to see the petition; it could not be found. He wishes to remember even the names of the three criminals, for the pardon bad been solicited and granted for the three; but notwithstanding all his efforts, he could only bring to mind one name, and that was Pellegrino Ruocco. At once, without any other formality, he orders one of his officers to carry to the telegraph the expression of the royal will; but the forgetting the names causing the forgetting the persons of the others, Pellegrino Ruocco is the only one of whom he recollects to announce the pardon. It was time for it to arrive. Already in Avellino all was in motion for the execution of the sentence; the criminals, taken from their prison, were advancing toward the place of execution, and were arriving at it the moment that the telegraphic dispatch appeared. It was an order from the king; the expression of the order was not clear. It bears but one word: "Let it be suspended." The director of the observatory fluctuates in irresolution. However, the announcement concerns the condemned, and there is not a moment to lose. He leaves a person in his stead; he goes to the place of execution, and in the king's name he commands a delay. The thing was so extraordinary that the officer of justice felt great difficulty in acting in accordance with this order, and they were discussing the matter with warmth, when the person left at the telegraph ran to them, and brought in clear and precise terms the entire pardon. Pellegrino is pardoned -- he alone. He had interested in his favor the powerful St. Philomena. The unhappy man was already upon the ladder; he was informed of his good fortune; he fell down, overpowered with joy. He soon recovered; liberty, honor, life are restored to him, all of which he owes to his bountiful protectress. My God, what cannot your goodness do! And in us, Christians, what may not the faith do which you have given us! We shall give some new examples. In the month of October, 1832, a violent tempest arose on the Adriatic Sea, and two fishing barks were wrecking in the very sight of port. As soon as the news ran through the town of Viesta, crowds flew to the sea-shore. The sight was terrific. Vain efforts were made to convey succor to the wretched mariners; the fury of the sea allowed none to reach them; they called, they cried out, their cries rent the hearts of those that heard them, and they answer them only by fruitless wishes, sighs, and lamentations. But the recollection of St. Philomena suddenly occurs, and revives hope in the despairing people. St. Philomena can do everything with God; she will save from death the unfortunate that implore her. A cry is immediately heard on all sides; the name of St. Philomena echoes in the clouds; a miracle is wrought. For some moments afterward the wretched fishermen were transported upon the shore without their perceiving it, and, together with their countrymen, they blessed her by whose unseen hand they had been saved from death. The prodigy was not, however, so complete that some fear and bitterness did not remain. The master of one of the barks, named Paul d'Aposto, in looking about, missed his two children, the youngest of whom was but eight years old. The raging billows had cast them far from the port. Some of the people on shore thought they could see them struggling with the waves, but who could give them any relief? She who had just given it with such wonderful success. "St. Philomena, finish your work; save these two poor children!" was the prayer that every heart made, and every mouth expressed. God willed, for the greater glory of his saint, that the same prayer should be made by one of the little unfortunates; it was the youngest, who, remembering in the midst of his danger the miraculous statue of St. Philomena placed in the church of the Capuchins, had recourse to her with confidence. "O new Virgin," cried he, "who art lately come to the Capuchins of Viesta, save us ; have pity on us." And while he struggled beside his brother against the waves, while his father was grieving on the shore, and the people, animated with a living confidence, persevered in their supplications to the saint, behold the children are saved; they come out of the midst of the foaming sea, and are safe in the port. The miracles wrought by the goodness of the Lord, and the power of his glorified servant, are proclaimed in acclamations of gratitude and joy.

Chapter VI. Examples of a just severity exercised by Saint Philomena against the impious.

A man and his wife, who lived at Montemarano, seeing themselves without posterity, had recourse to St. Philomena, and promised her if she obtained for them a daughter, to give it in baptism the name of Philomena, and to carry it immediately to Mugnano, there to return thanks to the saint. Their request was granted, and the first condition fulfilled; but as for the second, in spite of all her husband could say, his wife would never consent to it. Two years had passed away; the infant was handsome and amiable, and her parents idolized her; but, my God! what a disaster did their infidelity prepare for them! The report is circulated at Montemarano that there is to be a solemn fete in honor of St. Philomena at Castelvetere, a town a little distance off, and the mother immediately said to her husband that she would bring there the little Philomena, in order to accomplish, her vow. He answered that such was not the promise. "It is to Mugnano," said he, "not to Castelvetere, that you should bring the child." "Folly," replied his wife, "as if there was any difference between St. Philomena here and at Mugnano! Let us go . . ." She went there, and did not return home until evening, thinking she had payed her debt. Heaven judged otherwise, for the very same evening, at the moment that the little child, full of health, preparatory to going to bed, had kissed its parents, and called them in its own little language, they saw it expire in their arms. It is useless to trace here their sorrow and their grief. They proceeded at last, but too late, to Mugnano, where they related the tragical event. "It is," said they, "certainly our fault. This last but terrible blow had been preceded by many warnings, and even temporal pains, from which we were delivered by renewing our vow. We deferred, however, continually, and the patience of the Lord gave way to his justice. Oh, may he be satisfied with this afflicting chastisement!"

A rich man, who had likewise failed to fulfill his obligations, was punished in a terrible manner. He suffered from a cancer, which extended over his face, and had taken away a part of his nose. As soon as the blessed relics had arrived at Mugnano, he went to pray and bemoan his condition before them, promising, if he obtained his cure, to give to the saint one of the houses that he had. The miracle took place at the end of some days, during which he anointed often the diseased part with the oil of the lamp that burned before the shrine; not only the sore, but also the shocking deformity which was the consequence of it, totally disappeared; "and let us admire," says the author, an eye-witness of the fact, "this prodigy, doubly miraculous, inasmuch as the cure contained a sort of creation." Everyone expected the speedy fulfillment of the promise. The cured man, alone, thought of it no longer. At that period the chapel was building; its accomplishment would, therefore, have come in a seasonable time. Several persons put him in mind of his engagement; they even entreated his wife; but both answered coldly that it would be time enough after their death.... It appears that God took them at their word; bankruptcy came upon them, grief soon killed the wife, and her husband, reduced to the greatest wretchedness, and obliged to pay to one of his creditors rent for one of his own houses, became attacked again with the cancer, and it eat away his entire face, and shortly after deprived him of life. Happy for him if, before his death, he acknowledged his fault!

During several years a lawsuit was carried on between two noblemen who lived at Naples, and a village composed of poor farmers. The cause of the latter being the best, justice inclined in their favor, and they acknowledged that they owed this success more to the protection of St. Philomena than to the goodness of their cause. The final sentence was, however, not yet pronounced, and the two nobles, who were brothers, by the interest they possessed, and the springs they set in motion, were so far successful that the suit was decided in their favor. The news was almost, instantly carried to the little village, and spread consternation and mourning throughout it. The suit had already impoverished its inhabitants, and the loss of it deprived them of the necessary resources. What were they to do? If all hope from man was extinguished, they had still St. Philomena to look to; they laid before her, in tears, their case and their hopes. The noblemen heard of it, but, supported by the world's power, they

laughed at the simplicity of the villagers. "We shall see," said they to some of them, "what St. Philomena will do for you. Wait until we go to you, and you will tell us what she has availed you." Among the villagers there was a woman who had been particularly favored by St. Philomena; at these impious expressions she felt greatly hurt, and, transported with zeal, she exclaimed, "Gentlemen, do not outrage her whom you call our saint; she is more powerful than you; and woe to him who dares to provoke her wrath!" "What then will she do to us?" said they, laughingly. "What will she do to you? She could undoubtedly deprive you of life even before you set your foot in the village." To this they replied with laughter and expressions of contempt. The journey to the village was decided upon, and they departed like two vultures, about to pounce unerringly upon their prey. On the way they met several of the villagers, with whom their malice led them to be merry at the expense of St. Philomena. "Very well, very well," answered some of the villagers, "justice is on our side, interest and intrigue on yours. What could we do, after the loss of our cause, but to have recourse to our advocate? Beware of insulting her; she is as much above us as she is terrible in her vengeance."

Others, in terms more bold and clear merely said, "Gentlemen, no boasting; who knows whether you will arrive alive in the village?" These last words were repeated by several successively, who had neither heard nor seen each other, and were the foreboding of an approaching catastrophe; they were, however, replied to by laughter and mocking. There now remained but one village to pass before reaching the journey's end. The carriage was near being overturned at approaching this place, at which one of the brothers said to the other, "What a danger we have just escaped! I do not know what might have happened if the carriage had not recovered its balance." The driver heard the observation, but he to whom it was addressed answered nothing. The speaker, whom fear had seized, immediately felt his heart beat in an extraordinary manner, so that he became too bad to proceed farther, and was obliged to stop at the village to take some rest. In a short time he was a corpse, though but a few hours before enjoying vigorous health. This terrible blow made a strong impression on the second, who was of a stouter constitution than his brother; but who can resist the avenging sword that arms the saints? He, likewise, an instant after, fell a victim to the same hand, as he was guilty of the same impiety, and the same blasphemies. Thus were realized the prophetic threats of the oppressed villagers. They had, notwithstanding, their hearts so good, that, dissembling the injustice of these unhappy men against them, after their death they spoke advantageously of their other qualities. "I saw many of them," says Don Francis," come to Mugnano, to recommend the two deceased to the prayers of St. Philomena."

The following remarkable example of the punishment of impiety will conclude for the present the account of the miracles wrought through the power that God has been pleased, in His mercy, to communicate to the blessed St. Philomena: --

In a certain neighborhood there lived a very rich and powerful man, who only used his wealth and interest to harass and persecute every one about him. There was no one who had not to complain of his wickedness; and against every effort that had been made to reduce, by kindness or force, this little tyrant to his duty, he always found means to succeed. St. Philomena had just wrought in the same place a miracle, of which all the people and a great number of strangers had been witness. This man could not be witness himself, on account of his absence at the time it took place. When he returned, he heard the account; but he instantly exclaimed, "A lie! an imposture!" One might have called him a serpent spitting his venom. "Well," said the victims of his injustice, in the simplicity of their faith, "he now attacks the saint; we are indeed avenged;" and the report spread, somehow or other, that the unfortunate man would not see the fate of St. Philomena. The people all repeated it with one voice. The thing happened, in fact, according to the prediction: he died suddenly, "and his death, which took place before the fete" says our author, "bore visible and striking marks of a chastisement from Heaven. But it is not requisite to render them public."

Chapter VII. Practices of devotion in honor of St. Philomena.

The most solid practice, and, perhaps, the least used, of our devotion toward the saints, is that of which St. Augustin speaks. "Every time we honor the martyrs," says he, "let us not confine ourselves to asking, through their intercession, temporal benefits; but let us, by imitating their virtues, render ourselves worthy the enjoyment of eternal good. They are truly martyrs who endeavor to follow the martyrs' steps; for, could we, in truth, celebrate the glory of their martyrdom, without feeling ourselves urged to suffer like them? But, alas! we wish to share in their joy, without sharing in their sufferings; and by this means we shall see ourselves excluded from their happiness." * These words show us sufficiently the principal intention of the Lord and of His Church, in the worship we do to the saints; an intention clearly expressed in these terms by the eighth General Council, held at Nice: Ut nos sanctitudinis eorum fiamus participes; that is to say, that we should implore the intercession of the most pure and ever Virgin Mary, of the angels and of the saints; that we should salute and venerate the relics of the saints, in order to render us sharers in their holiness and virtues.

* *Sermon xlvii., on the Saints.*

Are we, then, anxious to interest particularly St. Philomena in our cause? Let us meditate on her life; let us contemplate her sufferings; let us reflect on the heroism of her death; and, applying to our state the virtues which have appeared to us the most important in her, let us take courage and extirpate from our hearts the vices or defects opposed to those virtues; let us strengthen, let us perfect the habit of the same virtues, by the purest and most frequent exercise of the acts that they produce.

First consideration.

Let me reflect, that St. Philomena lived in the world, and that I live in it too; and what is the vast difference between me and her? She was entirely detached from the world; I am chained to its maxims, its laws, its impure and ridiculous usages. Am I not bound to it by some affection that the Gospel has reproved? Am I not anxious to please worldlings -- to acquire their esteem? Do not my desires impetuously spring towards the seductive and dangerous pleasures which I see displayed by the vanity of the world? Ah! let us quit these bonds; let us abandon these reflections; let us extinguish these desires, let us aspire to more lasting consolation. St. Philomena, help me to honor thee: I wish to offer those sacrifices to God.

Second consideration.

St. Philomena lived in the midst of the world; I have the happiness of being removed from it. A thousand means of sanctification, which I have, and of which she was deprived, render to me more easy the practice of virtue and the shunning of vice. But what does my conscience tell me here? Where does it place me at these reflections? Can I bear the comparison between myself and the saint? And, as it turns out to my disadvantage, what conclusion am I to draw from it? Ah! Lord, forgive me the abuse of so many graces! Chastise me not, as the wicked and idle servant. I wish to be henceforward faithful and generous, to employ carefully the numberless ways that Thy divine bounty affords to me for making satisfaction.

I take this resolution, O St. Philomena, of imitating your example! Co-operate, I beseech you, by your prayers, in the efforts which I make.

Third consideration.

St. Philomena made a vow of virginity, and thus she annihilated the pleasures of the flesh and hopes that flatter. The vow absorbed, as it were, all her earthly futurity; it stripped of its brightest jewel the royal crown that was destined for her. "But what matters it?" said she to herself; "the whole world is nothing compared to the value of one degree of perfection that I shall give to my soul. It is better to belong entirely to God, than to divide our thoughts, our cares, between Him and creatures: there is more wisdom in flying from danger than in walking at the side of the abyss." What nobleness in the sentiment! what liveliness of faith! what generosity in such a sacrifice! God calls me, perhaps, on another way. I say, perhaps; have I seriously reflected on it? Ah! if this other way be not the way of the Lord, but only mine! or the way of interest! or that of an affection little in accordance" with the divine will! But, in fine, if I am still a virgin, do I carefully guard this valuable treasure? So many enemies, visible and invisible, endeavor to deprive me of it, or at least to diminish its perfection. Have I made for it a rampart by humility, by modesty, by prayer, and frequenting the sacraments, &c.? If I have formed in the world the sacred union of marriage, have I had for it the respect due to the elevation to which an august sacrament has raised it, &c.? O St. Philomena, watch over me from your height in heaven; watch over the sacred deposit of chastity that belongs to me. For your honor I will redouble my watchfulness, &c., &c.

Fourth consideration.

St. Philomena renounced the most attractive advantages of the world -- she truly comprehended the sense of the words of Solomon, "Vanity of vanities." And not satisfied with comprehending it, she knew how to reduce it to practice, at the most difficult but most glorious moment of her life. My God! what motives for confusion for me, in this admirable announcement! Miserable heart, feel shame that vanity captivates thee, and makes of thee a toy! By sacrificing all, St. Philomena became what she is. By seeking after all, thou hast deprived thyself of the good things which alone deserved thy esteem. Thou believest, perhaps, that the world, though poor as it is, has wherewithal to enrich those who serve it and that its ignominy (for has not God cursed it?) can lead you to true honor; that what it calls pleasures, and what brings to it only bitterness of heart, can bring to you happiness? Foolish being! your error is the more culpable, because it exposes you, with your own consent, to the greatest peril. For, is it not written, that the friends of the world are the enemies of God? because the world, with all it possesses, all it is, affords but only malice. It is, therefore, full time to undeceive ourselves, and to use the world as if we used it not -- that is, to despise all that it esteems, to attach ourselves to nothing that it loves. Forgive, O my God, my past folly! Help me, O St. Philomena, to rectify my judgment, to break off my attachments, and even to consent, cheerfully, to sacrifice everything, if God should be pleased to demand so much from me.

Fifth consideration

St. Philomena suffered cruel torments for God: she was young, delicate, and descended from kings, which, according to the world, exempted her from any kind of suffering; and she had only to conceal her religion: to do so, no reasons could apparently be more just or more urgent, the motive being nothing less than to protect her parents from the rage of Diocletian, and to save her own life. But St. Philomena remembered the express declaration of the Lord: "Whosoever does not hate his father, mother, and very life for love of me, cannot be my disciple." She, therefore, practised what she knew, and suffered long and agonizing tortures. What do I think of heroism like hers? have I even the germ of such in my heart? Perhaps my obedience to God is because it now costs nothing to nature or the flesh; hence it is, that as soon as either complain, even against the most essential precepts, I yield, abandoning the practices of piety the most serviceable to my soul, and I imagine for myself fantastic pretexts, which create a delusion, in order to free me from all kind of remorse. And can I believe, that by conducting myself in this manner, I shall come to a happy end? I cannot believe it; such an end is impossible. Our Lord calls those only happy who add practice to knowledge. If I am a Christian, I must appear so; and I can neither be, nor appear to be a Christian, if I do not faithfully follow Jesus Christ, bearing my cross, as he carried His. Let us, then, willingly suffer; let us fulfil our duties, though disagreeable they may be; let us trample on human considerations; let us show ourselves always, and in every place, generous and faithful Christians. I promise to become so, O my God! Grant me, I beseech thee, through the merits of St. Philomena, the grace to accomplish my resolution.

Sixth consideration

St. Philomena remained unshaken under the fiercest tortures, presenting a prodigy of virtue more admirable, more rare, than the former. Many have begun, but many have not persevered to the end. St. Philomena pursued her course to its termination. She had no reflection upon self, no considerations on her family, no hesitation on the brilliant offers the emperor made; she had neither regret, complaint, nor reproach. It was the fiat, "Let it be done," of her Saviour, in the Garden of Olives; it was that which secured forever her election and her vocation. Am I constant to my plans of sanctification, or am I of the number of those who live an hour for God, and a day for the world and for themselves? The Saviour compares them to reeds shaken by the wind, St. Paul declares them to be seized by folly. The Wise Man likens them to the most changing of all the stars: Stultus ut luna mutatur. "If you persevere not," says St. Bernard, "your combats will not be followed by victory;" and though you were conqueror, the laurel would not decorate your brow. Ah! my Lord, what shall I answer to thy justice? A thousand times have I begun with the spirit, and as often ended with the flesh. At one time I have wished to become virtuous, and at another time I have grown weary of being so. The moment after I have bid adieu to the world, I have stretched out to it again my hand; and almost as soon as I have trampled on its vanities, I have bound myself again in its chains. Deplorable inconstancy! worthless desire! O my God, remove this changeableness of my inclinations, and fickleness of my thoughts! St. Philomena, obtain for me perseverance in good, since that only can save.

Seventh consideration.

St. Philomena was powerfully aided by God in her combats, and this is a proof of what St. Paul says: " God will proportion his succor to the violence of the temptations, in order that you may resist them." And what was this succor? Jesus himself -- and Jesus in the arms of his mother -- Mary -- the holy angels -- and the Spirit of Strength, which descended into the heart of the youthful Philomena. Thus might she exclaim with David, "The Lord watches over the preservation of my spiritual life; before whom shall I tremble? Though I should see whole legions united to my executioners, I would still hope. My God, you are with me." She could then pass, with fearless courage, through torments, and dare those who inflict them. O St. Philomena, will not God do also for me what he did for you? Am I not his child, like you? Alas! why should I harbor discouraging doubts? Why fear being abandoned? Has not the Spirit of Truth said, "Blessed is the man who suffers temptation?" The same Spirit has put these expressions in the mouth of St. Paul: "I glory in my sufferings ; in putting my fidelity to trial, they fill me with hope, and hope never deceives." Away, then, with these vain and unjust fears! In my tribulations I will call upon my God; in the tempest I will cast in his bosom the sure anchor of unshaken confidence. O holy protectress, strengthen me in these sentiments.

Eighth consideration.

St Philomena withstood victoriously the attacks made upon her, and it was death upon the field of battle that procured for her eternal blessedness; a crown more glorious than that of all the princes in the world; and palms, such as were never gathered by the greatest conquerors. She overcame shame and suffering; both united in vain their efforts to subdue her. Glory covers her like a garment. Raise thy voice, O illustrious martyr! reproach now thy proud enemies; tell them with the Apostle, "Shame and pain, where now is our victory? what has become of the sting of your arrows, of the sharpness of your swords, of the stamp of disgrace and infamy that you attempted to set on my forehead? I died, and I live; I conquered, and I triumph; I was dragged to the scaffold, and now behold me glorified in heaven." Thus humiliation is the forerunner of glory; the cross is the pledge of happiness. Have I comprehended it? Do I wish to come to the practice of it? Should I have to support the efforts of the most terrible enemies, to engage in a combat of blood, how long could it last? What sort of a fight would it be? Momentaneum et leve, says St. Paul; a moment, a slight contest, almost nothing; and then, aeterum gloriae pondus; a weight of glory, but a weight the value of which measures an eternity! O my heart, expand thyself at this hope; not only thou shalt be resigned in thy different trials, but thou shalt exult with joy at them. I sow, thou shalt say, but what a lovely harvest do I secure! Scepters and crowns I shall one day reap. Let my tears flow, since to them is promised so valuable a consolation. Sorrows, avoid me not, as after ye the sweetest joys will come! Let me embrace you, O penance, O mortification, as you are the germ of a glorious resurrection. Yes, I desire to suffer in order to enjoy; I wish to fight, in order to conquer. I wish to humble myself and to be humbled, that my God may exalt me; I wish to die to the world, to sin, to myself, that I may live to

God, in God, and with God, for all eternity. St. Philomena, draw me after you, and aid me by your intercession, as you have enlightened and animated me by your example.

Ninth consideration.

Saint Philomena appears in the church militant in order to exercise a glorious apostleship. The works of the just perish not. They are seeds that remain buried for a time, but the day comes when they become a tree, crowned with blossoms and fruit: life is their winter of which death terminates the chill, that is succeeded by a sun which will shine through eternity. The voice that will call the just to the enjoyment of heaven, will summon them in these words: "Now the winter is past, the clouds are gone; get up, my friend, and come." The just will spring up at the words, and appear at once among the dwellers of heaven, like "a vine clothed in leaves and fruit ;" like a flower, as lovely in the brilliancy of its color as in the beauty of its shape; and the celestial host, on beholding them, will unanimously proclaim, "A flower has shown itself in our gardens, a new vine sends us its fragrance; come, come, O holy and dearly-beloved soul!" take thy place in the midst of us; and thus it is the Just One "enters into his glory." But this is not enough; the earth, that has sent this present to heaven, will it have no mark of gratitude? It shall, and this mark will be an abundance of new graces, a dew, as it were, of visible and invisible benedictions. Let us look for the evidence of this in

St. Philomena. Are not her merits still living, though many ages have passed by? Are they not superabundantly applicable as to astonish the world? What hast thou done, O Philomena, to acquire this glory? "She loved justice and hated iniquity." Her heart, filled with affection for "the law of God," was fed with it night and day; and now, as the tree planted beside the waters, it yields its fruit. Everything she undertakes is crowned with success. Rejoice, then, O ye just, in the Lord; praise him when you remember the favors he has bestowed on you, and of which you have profited so well. Cannot I form myself after your example, in order to take part one day in your fruitfulness? I will begin, at last, to follow you. I now set about sowing my ground with acts of virtue; and the more the seed is abundant, the greater will be the harvest. Let us draw, then, abundantly out of the treasures of "piety, patience, charity, obedience," and of all Christian virtues. Let us seek only God in our least actions. Let us profit by every grace. Let us amass, let us treasure up, for the church of heaven, and the church on earth. What I do for God, I do for myself, for the angels, for the saints, for the just, for sinners. Let us make haste; let us not lose a moment. Aid me, O St. Philomena, and you also will share in my harvest.

In proposing to our readers the foregoing considerations, we only intended to facilitate the means of obtaining the most beneficial effects from devotion towards the saints. And if anyone should desire to see more particularly specified those acts, which the saint seems to suggest, by her virtues and her works, the following detail may help to show what may be advantageously practised in her honor: --

1. To keep a stricter watch over our eyes.

2. To forbid ourselves all useless conversations and visits.

3. To banish all superfluity, all unbecoming manner of dress.

4. To deprive ourselves of everything that flatters nature and the senses.

5. To cut off everything unlawful in our affections.

6. To draw somewhat nearer to God by prayer and meditation.

7. To gain some signal victory over human respect.

8. To betake ourselves with more zeal to works of Christian charity.

9. To distinguish in our care and affection the poor and children.

10. To imitate the simple in their devotion towards the saints.

A piety, truly enlightened, cannot fail to appreciate these practices; it will add others to them, and will more and more merit the favor of God and of St. Philomena. *

Quin potius majora his offeratis, et qualia eos decent, qui sanctos rite venerantur, corporis nempe exinanitionem, animae elevationem, pravitatis declinationem, virtutis incrementum. S. Greg. Naz.

Prayers.

In regard of prayers, we shall also insert some here, which are within the comprehension of all. We shall, however, preface them by the following considerations: "If any person," says the Council of Trent, "has the impiety to teach that we ought not to invoke the saints, who enjoy in heaven eternal beatitude; that they do not pray to God for men ; that to have recourse to their intercession is an idolatry condemned by the law of God, and opposed to the honor of Jesus Christ, the only mediator between God and man, let him be Anathema. * The Catholic, Apostolic, and Roman Church, agreeing in this, both with tradition and the practices of the first Christians, and with the rules established by holy councils, teaches, that on the contrary, the saints, who reign with Jesus Christ, offer their prayers to God for men, that it is good and useful to invoke them humbly, and that, in order to obtain graces from God, through Jesus Christ his Son, our Lord, who is alone our Redeemer, and our Saviour, it is advantageous to have recourse to their prayers, to their power, to their intercession." What the mother teaches, the true children have ever practised. Let us hear St. Basil, speaking of the forty martyrs: "Let him, whose soul tribulations plunge into anguish, implore their succor, and let him be imitated by those whose heart is in joy; the first will ask his deliverance, the latter the perpetuity of their happiness. Let us pour our desires and our prayers into the bosoms of the martyrs." And in giving the example himself, lie exclaims, "O holy company! O sacred battalion! O ye common protectors of the human race! you who so willingly share in all our solicitudes; who support, by your suffrages, our prayers and our wishes; you, powerful ambassadors, whom the earth has deputed to God, stars of the universe, flowers of the churches, pray for us."

If we listen to St. Gregory Nazianzen addressing St. Cyprian, we shall hear him speak thus: "Cast upon us, from the height of heaven, a favorable look; direct our words and our life; unite yourselves to us, to feed and govern these flocks, to defend them against the biting of the wolves." And then, as if to justify the confidence he has in the intercession of the holy martyr, "Cyprian," says he, "is all-powerful; the dust of his bones, that even of his tomb, if we venerate them with faith, enjoy the same power." They who have made the trial with faith, know it by the miracles that have rewarded them.

St. Ephrem, supplicating the martyrs, addresses them in this manner: "O you, who, for your Master and Saviour, faced such torments with such generosity; yon, whom an intimate familiarity unites to the Lord in all things, we beseech you to vouchsafe to intercede with him for our necessary wants and our negligences. Ask for our hearts the grace of Jesus, a ray of his sacred love, which, in enlightening our souls, may make them burn with the fire of the most ardent charity." Let us hear, finally, St. Bernard, opening his soul to the soul of the martyr, Victor: "O hero," he cries out,

"who, after having supported the fatigue of the severest combat, now enjoyest the repose and happiness of the angels; look upon these timid, these cowardly brothers in arms, who, finding themselves surrounded by hostile swords, are engaged in singing thy praises! O illustrious conqueror! who hast known how to triumph over earth, and at the same time to conquer heaven, in disdaining with a holy pride the glory of the first, and in offering to the latter a pious violence, cast thy eyes upon us, poor captives, and may our victory, the effect of thy succor, come as a conclusion to thy trophies! What consolation, O Victor! what sweetness, what delight, in honoring thee, in singing to thee, in praying to thee, in this place of affliction, in this body of death. Thy name, thy remembrance, are a honeycomb that melts upon my lips. Come, then, courageous combatant, amiable protector, faithful advocate; arise to succor us; thy succor will be to us a happiness, and to thyself a new glory."

Such were the prayers of the saints to other saints; why should poor sinners like us not imitate their example? Is it because we have been and that we are still in the bonds of sin? "No, no," cries out to us St. Ambrose, a faithful echo of the doctrine of Jesus Christ; "if the fever of sin devours you, do not fail to have recourse to the saints. Ally yourselves by prayer with the apostles, the martyrs, the angels themselves, and the Divine mercy will draw near to you. A heart enslaved to sin can certainly do less than the heart of the just man, to obtain for itself, by prayer, the graces that it requires but it has intercessors with the heavenly Physician, who make up for this deficiency. Pray, therefore, to the holy angels; pray to the holy martyrs; be not ashamed to employ, in aid of your own weakness, those who have perhaps had to wash away weakness in their blood; pray to them; they can pray for your sins." *

* *In libro de Viduis.*

This is what we are going to do, in depositing at the feet and in the heart of St. Philomena our prayers and our desires. Amongst the most usual practices in Italy, are novenas or nine days' prayers, and triduum or three days' prayers, which are celebrated with much external grandeur, and great devotion. Generally, for the latter, the august Sacrament was exposed, at least during the entire exercise appointed in honor of the saint; for our Lord Jesus Christ loves to unite with his church in the triumph of his elect. In the morning, they had a solemn mass; in the evening, the grand salutation, * after the panegyric of St. Philomena. The altar, where was placed the picture of the saint, with a relic, was richly adorned, and lighted with a great number of wax candles; and towards it, during almost every hour of the day, a multitude of the faithful were seen pressing their way. Some offered to God, by the hands of their advocate, only the prayer of the heart; others recited, with faith and humility, their beads; several read, with recollected devotion, the little book containing the novena of St. Philomena.

* *Prayers sung by the choir in the evening after the office, and benediction of the Blessed Sacrament*

The heart, particularly in matters connected with prayer, desires a holy liberty. God comprehends all languages. We know, however, that he prefers a fervent briefness to

long prayers which do not animate true devotion. It would be perhaps better to let each one determine the time and the form of his prayers; but, as we do not pretend to impose laws upon any, one, it may be permitted us to trace out a little plan, which people may adopt if they wish, in performing either the three days' prayers, or the novena, in honor of St. Philomena.

1st. Ornament as well as you can a little oratory, and place in it an image or relic of the saint; both, if you have them.

2dly. During this time, keep, if you can, a lamp continually lighted, before the image or relic. This will be, as it were, a mark of your devotion, and of your confidence in the saint; your heart, of which it will be the symbol, will animate it with the breath of a living faith. More than one miracle has been wrought by means of the oil of these lamps.

3dly. If you perform two exercises during the day, you will be able, during the first, to meditate on some one of the virtues and miracles of St. Philomena; and you will draw from them conclusions to be practised for the amendment of your heart and life. You will conclude it by reciting the litany of the ever blessed Virgin, and repeat thrice the two verses, Regina martyrum, Regina Virginum, ora pro nobis. You will add, at the end, "Pray for us, O St. Philomena! that we may be made worthy of the promises of Christ."

Prayer.

Grant, O Lord, I beseech thee, that the Virgin and Martyr, St. Philomena, may solicit thy mercy for us. I implore her intercession, through the merits of her chastity, and by the glory that she gave to thy power, in dying for thee. I beseech thee, O my God, through Jesus Christ, our Lord, who lives and reigns with thee eternally, in unity with the Holy Ghost. Amen.

In the second exercise, which will be perhaps sufficient for a great number of persons, who are too much occupied to perform two, there may be read, at first, some pages of this little book, which may be reflected on for some moments; and the conclusion may be made by the following prayer:--

Prayer to St. Philomena.

O faithful Virgin and glorious Martyr, who vouchsafest from heaven, where you are, to pour down so great a number of benefits upon the earth, I bless the Lord for the graces he bestowed on yon during your life, and above all, at your death; I glorify him and praise him for the honor and the power with which he crowns you today.

Blessed be thou, O holy God! O God, adorable in thy saints! O just God! O powerful God! O God of infinite mercy!

O faithful Virgin and glorious Martyr, whose faith triumphed over all the attacks of the world and of hell, I bless God for your triumphs; I praise him and I give him glory for the victorious strength he communicated to you.

Blessed be thou, O holy God! O God, adorable in thy saints! O just God! O powerful God! O God of infinite mercy!

O faithful Virgin and glorious Martyr, who did prefer to the visible goods of this world, the invisible but measureless treasures of a blessed eternity, I bless God for the firm hope that he put in your heart; I praise him and glorify him for the victory which he caused you to gain over the tempter and over yourself.

Blessed be thou, O holy God! O God, adorable in thy saints! O just God! O powerful God !O God of infinite mercy!

O faithful Virgin and glorious Martyr, the raging waters of tribulation that rolled over you, were unable to extinguish the charity that consumed your soul; I bless God for the constancy he gave you; I praise him and I give him glory for this noble ardor, that made you devour, as it were, so many sufferings.

Blessed be thou, O holy God! O God, adorable in thy saints! O just God! O powerful God! O God of infinite mercy!

O faithful Virgin and glorious Martyr, whose powerful arm fights this day for the church upon earth, I bless God for the choice by which he has honored you: I praise him and I glorify him for the numberless wonders of which he makes you the agent, and of which the Catholic, Apostolic, and Roman Church gathers the fruits.

Blessed be thou, O holy God! O God, adorable in thy saints! O just God! O powerful God of infinite mercy!

O faithful Virgin and glorious Martyr, I rejoice at your glory; I am filled with gladness at seeing the glory you render to God, particularly by the miracles wrought in favor of the poor and simple: I pray the Divine Majesty to make known your name more and more, to show forth your power, and to multiply the number of your devoted servants.

Blessed be thou, O holy God! O God, adorable in thy saints! O just God! O powerful God of infinite mercy!

O faithful Virgin and glorious Martyr, have compassion on me; exercise upon my soul and upon my body the ministry of salvation, of which God has judged you worthy; you know better than I the multitude and variety of my wants; behold me at your feet, full of poverty and hope; I solicit your charity, O great Saint! hear me graciously; bless me; vouchsafe to render agreeable to my God, the humble petition which I present to you (here one may specify the favor they desire to obtain from the saint). Yes, I have the firm hope, that through your merits, through your ignominy, through your death, united to the merits of the death and passion of our Lord Jesus

Christ, I shall obtain what I ask of you, and I will say, in the joy of my heart,

Blessed be thou, O holy God! O God, adorable in thy saints! O just God! O powerful God of infinite mercy!

Pater and Ave for the Pope and for the necessities of the church.

Another novena to Saint Philomena.

First day.

Consider that Saint Philomena was a virgin and always pure, in the midst of the world, in spite of persecution even to death. What a model! Can I contemplate it without feeling humbled? and knowing the cause of my confusion, what should be the remedy?

Practice. -- 1st. Hear the holy mass in her honor, and visit one of her statues or images, if such can be done conveniently. 2d. Humble yourself several times, for whatever, in the course of your life, may have tarnished the purity of your soul.

This Novena is usually made from the 1st to the 10th of August, which is the day of the martyrdom and translation of the Saint; but it may be said at any other time.

Second day.

Consider that St. Philomena was constantly pure and innocent, because she knew how to mortify her inclinations, and to observe in all her deportment the modesty of Jesus Christ, to keep away from a perverse world, and from dangerous occasions. Do you imitate her in this holy vigilance?

Practice. -- 1st. As on the first day. 2d. Avoid what has injured you; practice what you have neglected, and what will preserve you always pure and agreeable in the eyes of the Lord.

Third day.

Consider that St. Philomena preserved and increased her love of perfect purity by means of prayer, the abundant source of spiritual life; by the sacraments, wherein the soul is purified in the blood of Jesus Christ, and is nourished with his sacred body, the divine germ of Christian virginity; by the recollection that her members belonged to Jesus Christ, and that her body was the temple of the Holy Ghost. Have not you the same means? What use do you make of them?

Practice, -- Ist. As on the first day. 2d. Recite all your prayers with increased fervor; say to yourself, from time to time: I belong to Jesus Christ, I am the temple of the Holy Ghost.

Fourth day.

Consider that St. Philomena was a martyr, that she had to suffer -- to suffer a great deal, even death itself; and that she displayed in her torments, invincible patience. Do you suffer with the like patience? You have, perhaps, but seldom to suffer; and are never in danger of death from suffering. Whence comes so much weakness? What means will you take to acquire patience?

Practice, -- 1st. As on the first day. 2d. Suffer patiently the few afflictions, contradictions, and trials, with which the Lord may please to visit you on this day.

Fifth day.

Consider that St. Philomena suffered martyrdom for Jesus Christ: endeavors were made to deprive her of faith, to make her violate her baptismal vows, to induce her to follow the example of idolaters or apostates. And do not the devil, the world, the flesh, and your own heart endeavor to lead you into the like sins?

Do not imprudent fears make yon fail in your duties, and violate your sacred engagements? What shameful pusillanimity! Let us resume, at length, courage to perform our duty to God.

Practice. -- 1st. As on the first day. 2d. Obtain some victory over mere human respect: say to yourself. It is better to please God than men.

Sixth day.

Consider that St. Philomena had to put in practice this word of our Saviour: "He who does not hate his very life for sake of me, cannot be my disciple." She hesitated not to sacrifice all, her very life, for the love of Christ. In occasions far less difficult, do we show ourselves worthy of Jesus Christ? If there be a competition between God and man, between grace and nature, between the love of God and human affections, to which do we give the preference? Oh, let us never more degenerate from our dignity of children of God, and of disciples? of Jesus Christ.

Practice. -- 1st. As on the first day. 2d. Endeavor to please only God, or creatures for God alone. Remove far from you every inordinate affection.

Seventh day.

Consider that St. Philomena in her martyrdom had to suffer raillery, sarcasm, outrages, and such like painful treatment, from her persecutors, from her executioners, and from the greater part of the spectators of her cruel sufferings: she was not, however, the less generous, the less constant, or less joyful in the public confession of her faith. Should the world give you to drink of the cup of affliction, will you have the courage to drink of it with similar sentiments? But what signify contempt, disdain, and even persecutions the most unjust and bloody? Can he whom God esteems, can he ever be, or can he ever think himself dishonored? Fear not, O Christian heart; continue your journey, which will end in eternal glory.

Practice. -- 1st. As on the first day. 2d. Do not let your heart be disturbed, if there be said today any sharp, rude, or offensive word, &c.

Eight day.

Consider that St. Philomena, by dying, for our Lord Jesus Christ, to all things here on earth, entered into the joy of eternal life. "Yes, I am certain," she would say, in her heart, "that the Sovereign Judge will render unto me, for the perishable goods which I sacrifice to his love, the crown of justice he has promised me." She dies, and forthwith this worthy spouse of Jesus Christ shines in the tabernacle of God, with those who accompany the Lamb. Are. these the thoughts which I entertain when there is question of making any sacrifice for God? "What impression do they make upon my heart? To what side do they make it incline? The saint says. To have all, let us lose all. What do I say?

Practice, -- 1st. As on the first day. 2d. Impose upon yourself some voluntary sacrifice. Perform with promptitude, and with a good heart, all the duties belonging to your condition of life.

Ninth day.

Consider that St, Philomena, for having sacrificed everything here on earth for Jesus Christ, receives from him, even in this world, more than a hundred-fold. How great is her renown, how powerful her intercession! how numerous the supplications made through her to the throne of mercy! What devout veneration is paid to her statues and pictures, and what zealous anxiety to obtain her relics! It is thus that

God accomplishes his promises. Oh, that we would fulfil, with equal fidelity, the promises we have made to God! But by our infidelity to God, we deprive ourselves of much merit and of many favors, both for this life and for the next. Let us take courage. Let us be faithful to God, and thus be made worthy of the promises of Christ.

Practice. -- 1st. As on the first day. 2d. Do today some work of mercy in honor of St. Philomena. Prepare yourself, by a good confession, to receive worthily our Lord Jesus Christ.

A prayer in honor of St. Philomena for each day of the novena.

Glorious Virgin and Martyr, beloved of God, blessed Philomena, I heartily rejoice and give God thanks, that he has given you so much power, for the glory of his name, for the edification of his church, and to honor the merits of your life and of your death. I am happy to see you so great, so pure, so generous, so faithful to Jesus Christ, and to the precepts and counsels of his gospel, and so highly rewarded both in heaven and on earth. Attracted by your example to the practice of sterling virtues, full of hopes at the view of the rewards bestowed upon your merits, I purpose to follow you in the avoidance of all evil, and in the fulfilment of God's commandments. Assist me, O glorious saint, by your powerful intercession, and obtain especially for me, a perfect purity, a fortitude invincible in all sorts of attacks, a generosity which refuses not to God anything whatsoever, and a love, stronger than death, for the faith of Jesus Christ, a ready and willing obedience to the holy Roman Catholic Church, and to our Sovereign Pontiff, the common father of all the faithful, the pastor of pastors and of their flocks, and vicegerent of Jesus Christ throughout the universe.

To these favors which I have now asked through your intercession, blessed Philomena, I also ask other new graces, which I have the fullest confidence to obtain through your powerful intercession. (Here declare those graces to the saint with simplicity, confidence, and humility.) Surely God, who is so good, and for whom you have given up your life; God, who is so good, and who has bestowed so many gifts and favors, both upon you, and through you; this God, who is so good as to have died for me, and to give himself to me in the eucharistic form, surely he will not refuse to attend graciously to your prayers, to my entreaties, and even to that necessity, which he himself, in some sort, feels to do us good. Thus, I hope; I put all my confidence in God and in you. Amen.

O Jesus, grant me grace to love thee, and to make others love thee. O Mary, my tender mother, obtain for us a great love for Jesus Christ.

Prayers

To implore her powerful protection in the tribulations, the temptations, and in all the necessities of life.

O MOST blessed St. Philomena! the Thaumaturga of our age, behold me prostrate before that throne, upon which the most adorable Trinity has placed and crowned you with the double crown of virginity and martyrdom. I raise my hands in supplication to yon. What a glorious spectacle in constancy and strength did yon not present, before heaven, and to earth, to angels and men, at the time that the tyrants of the world persecuted the sheep of the Savior, and deluged the church with their blood! The heavy anchor tied to your neck, even the waters into which yon were cast, shook not for an instant the fidelity yon had sworn to your heavenly Spouse. The merciless hand of the executioner rending, with its murderous lash, your virginal flesh, from which your pure blood gushed forth, extorted from you neither a tear nor a sigh. The arrows, the chains, the sword that perfected your sacrifice, and placed your sweet soul in the possession of glory, were unable to abate, even for a moment, the ardor of your generous heart, for your Divine Lover. Now, the Lord, in recompense of your anguish for the glory of that lily that you preserved inviolate, amidst the thorns of the world, and to the confusion of this corrupted age, has vouchsafed to glorify you, by the power of your intercession. From the east to the west, from the north to the south, the fame of your wonders is heard; the people crowd to seek refuge under the wings of your protection.

It is therefore to you, O illustrious martyr, it is to you that I have recourse; I stretch out to you my suppliant hands. Ah! from the height of the celestial country, vouchsafe to cast a look upon me, your humble servant. O pure virgin! O holy martyr, Philomena, comfort me in my afflictions; strengthen me in temptations; preserve me in persecutions; aid me in all dangers; but above all, aid me at the terrible hour of death, when I shall have to fight with all the powers of hell, and when a dreadful moment shall decide my eternity. In these days of darkness protect the church, which the impious attack with open force; baffle the designs of the wicked, and maintain the faithful in the unity of the Catholic Church, Amen.

For Monday,

Most pure virgin, most faithful disciple of the Gospel, and invincible martyr of Jesus Christ, whom God adorned with so many graces, with purity; who were enriched with so lively a faith, and such singular force, in the very midst of an infidel and corrupted world, and particularly at Rome, at that time the center of idolatry, of tyranny, of infernal superstition, and the school of the most enormous vices; O blessed Philomena, who at this pagan and corrupted head of the world, preserved for yourself an unshaken faith and inviolable purity to your last breath, sacrificing to your Spouse, in the most painful sufferings, your life, we beseech you, by the distinction of your merits, to obtain for us, at the merciful throne of our heavenly Father, the gift of perseverance in faith, of purity of mind and body, and a holy death in the grace of Jesus Christ. Amen.

For Tuesday.

O courageous martyr and most faithful virgin of Jesus Christ! to preserve unsullied the treasure of purity and of faith in your God, you suffered yourself to be cast, with an anchor tied to your neck, into the waters of the Tiber, from which your heavenly Spouse delivered you unhurt; we claim your intercession, to the end, that in the midst of the waters of bitterness, of anxieties, and of tribulations, which unceasingly surround us, we may be supported with strength, and preserved from the shipwreck of our sins, and from the death of our souls ; and that we may not be sunk by the waters of temptation. Amen.

For Wednesday.

O beloved spouse and fearless martyr of Jesus Christ! to preserve your virginity, your heroic faith made you endure with constancy, ignominious sufferings in the presence of a great number of vicious pagans, in the streets of idolatrous Rome. Besides, for the glory of virginity, and of the evangelical doctrine, you renounced the pleasures of the flesh, the de- lights and pomp of the world, and even the life of your chaste body. You suffered also the cruel scourging with iron-loaded lashes, which, in covering you with wounds, made you resemble that Jesus whom you so ardently loved. Alas! we confess ourselves wretched sinners, sensual and delicate worldlings; obtain for us the strength to enable us to live far removed from the mire of sin, and to die with courage, like you, in the faith of the Roman Church, though to do so should cost us suffering, disgrace, and even life itself. Amen.

For Thursday.

O courageous Virgin! who, with a supernatural joy and invincible force, thrice sacrificed your virginal body, in order to persevere in the doctrine of Christ, and defended heroically your virginity and faith; who esteemed yourself happy to be three times pierced with darts; who received as many palms and crowns as your body did wounds, for your heavenly Spouse, pray for us, who observe so indifferently the law of God; obtain for us the strength necessary to come to eternal salvation, to the end that we may bear with resignation the pains, the sorrows of this life, and that we may resist all the attacks of hell. Amen.

For Friday.

Illustrious martyr, and glorious spouse of Jesus Christ, who, being God and Saviour, permitted you not to be overcome, but having designed for you a distinguishing crown, prolonged your life, which, multiplying your sufferings, afforded the means of adding to your laurels and triumphs, and rendered you more admirable in the eyes of the celestial spirits, and more exalted amongst the glorious martyrs. By the divine counsel you were loaded anew with chains, and carried before the tribunal of the tyrants of Rome; your angelic purity and holy faith were put to new trials, and your barbarous enemies, despairing of conquering the heroic firmness of your heart, condemned you to be beheaded -- your final suffering, which, by filling up the measure of your merits, introduced you triumphant and glorious into the kingdom of your Spouse. Amen.

For Saturday.

We beseech you, O great saint, to cast upon us a look of charity. Vouchsafe to show us, by some mark of your goodness, that our humble homage has been grateful to you. Obtain for us the graces we desire for our salvation, as well as those which you see we require, in order to be delivered from the eternal death we have so often deserved. Grant that, in this hope, we may be freed from all troubles, that is, that your sweet charity may animate and console us. We bless with our whole heart, and with the most profound adoration, the most Holy Trinity, for having loaded you with so many benedictions on earth, for having adorned you with so much purity, with faith and with strength, for having exalted you to such high sanctity, and for having supported you in the midst of your enemies, and of such horrible sufferings, and conducted you in triumph to glory in heaven. We give thanks to the most pure Virgin Mary, Mother of God, Queen of Martyrs, who, like a tender mother, comforted you by her powerful protection in the midst of your torments. We hope, O holy martyr, that you yourself will protect us, now that we honor your merits and your glorious triumph. Amen,

Litany In Honor Of Saint Philomena.

Lord, have mercy on us.

Christ, have mercy on ns.

Lord, have mercy on us.

Christ, hear ns.

Christ, graciously hear us.

God the Father, of heaven, have mercy on us.

God the Son, Redeemer of the world, have mercy on us.

God the Holy Ghost, have mercy on us. Holy Trinity, have mercy on us.

Holy Mary, Queen of Martyrs, {Response: pray for us.}

St. Philomena, child of benediction,

St. Philomena, who wast the daughter of light,

St. Philomena, who from thy childhood chose Jesus Christ for thy spouse,

St. Philomena, who despisedst, with heroical courage, the greatest honors, in order to continue faithful to Jesus Christ,

St. Philomena, whose faith and love for Jesus Christ promises and threats could not change,

St. Philomena, whose constancy, neither the entreaties of a father, nor the tenderness of a mother could diminish,

St. Philomena, who, for thy great love of God in sufferings, deservedst to be consoled by Jesus and Mary,

St. Philomena, whose eagerness to endure new torments daily increased,

St. Philomena, whom God intrusted to the guardianship of angels, and who, by their aid, many times overcamest the fury of thy persecutors,

St. Philomena, whose glory God has been pleased to manifest by continual miracles,

St. Philomena, who sufferedst many kinds of martyrdom in the various torments thou hadst to endure,

St. Philomena, whose example attracted many to the faith,

St. Philomena, who, like Jesus, wast bound to a pillar and scourged,

St. Philomena, perfect model of Christian virgins,

St. Philomena, who protectest in a particular manner those who honor thee,

St. Philomena, whom the church honors and reveres as an illustrious virgin and martyr of Jesus Christ,

St. Philomena, who enjoyest a neverending glory,

Lamb of God, who bearest away the sins of the world, forgive us, O Lord. Lamb of God, who bearest away the sins of the world, graciously hear us, O Lord. Lamb of God, who bearest away the sins of the world, have mercy on us, O Lord.

PRAYER.

O glorious virgin and martyr, whose glory God has been pleased to make known by singular miracles, we address ourselves to thee with entire confidence. Obtain for us, that, by thy example, we may fight courageously against whatever is opposed to the reign of Jesus Christ in our hearts; that we may adorn them with virtue like thine, with that angelical purity, of which thou art a perfect model; and that, inflamed with the love of Jesus, we may continually walk in the way which he has marked out, to the end that we may one day partake of thy everlasting happiness, through our Lord Jesus Christ, who, with the Father and the Holy Ghost, liveth and reigneth one God, in perfect Trinity, for ever and ever. Amen.

THE END.

Electronic Book edited and typographically corrected for SaintsBooks.net

Made in the USA
Las Vegas, NV
25 January 2022